Manifestations of Mind in Matter

Iebele Abel

Manifestations of Mind in Matter

Conversations about
Art, Science, and Spirit

Manifestations of Mind in Matter.
Conversations about Art, Science, and Spirit.
© 2008, 2010, 2013, Iebele Abel
ISBN 1936033070

This work was first published in English as *Talks about Mind over Matter*,
Elmtree & Waters Publishers, The Hague, 2010

Keywords: art, philosophy, physics, religion, spirituality

ICRL Press
211 N. Harrison St., Suite C
Princeton, NJ 08540-3530

Contents

Introduction

A quote, attributed to Hermes Trismegistus in the Tabula Smaragdina,[1] reads: "As below, so above and as above, so below." This sentence in its original form is thousands of years old:

> There is nothing in which God doesn't live, because where heaven is, there is God, and where the world is, there is heaven also. I think God is in heaven and heaven is in the world.[2]

Are physical and spiritual realities really connected inseparably? That is the question under discussion in this book. And if this is the case, why do we experience a difference between the spiritual world and the reality we perceive with our senses?

Reality, perception, and consciousness are intertwined in a mysterious way. We have become used to the idea that everything in life happens according to the laws of cause and effect. The causal world view, however, is not appropriate for all experiences and perceptions. The exact sciences frequently encounter issues that are inconsistent with our causal assumptions.

Cause and effect are in no way self-evident in art either. The source of inspiration is often a mystery, and the insights that develop during the process of creation are not easy to interpret. Art originates through perception and thinking about perception. It does not differ substantially from science in this sense. In both disciplines, perception and thinking pose new questions again and again; questions that, so it seems, never let themselves be answered completely. As soon as a new perspective is taken, one's perception and one's manner of reflection change as well. The reality

---

1 This is one of the most influential texts in the history of alchemy.
2 Roelof van den Broek, Hermes Trismegistus, Amsterdam, Bibliotheca Philosophica Hermetica.

as we experience it obviously is not fixed, however much we try to notice structures and patterns in our perceptions. The study of our reality, whether in art, science, or daily life, resembles an eternal game in which every assumption is exchanged for a new one at a certain moment. And maybe — this is another possibility we will discuss in this book — physical reality only exists as a result of the image we create of it. Are we *co-creators* of the world we live in? In philosophy, this thought dates from times immemorial:

> Tat: "Is there a real reality on earth, after all, Father?"

> Hermes: "You are mistaken, my boy. Nowhere on earth, Tat, is there a true reality and there can't be, either. But some people, namely those whom God has given the ability to see, can visualize it."

Texts like these still have not lost their relevance to this day. Beyond that, growing numbers of people are, once again, contemplating the meaning that Hermes' ancient knowledge may have in their lives.

Several centuries of trying to describe reality in a deterministic way lie behind us. This materialistic, causal model offered little space for spirit in a framework that tried to understand everything in a concrete, tangible way. A concept like 'God' is too vague in such a model, so it gradually disappeared altogether from scientific thinking. God, and spirituality became an obsolete, or at best, an irrelevant concept.

But not everything in the world conforms to the laws of cause and effect. At the beginning of the twentieth century, quantum mechanics introduced the idea that something exists only when it is perceived. Other scientific research provided evidence that human consciousness seemed capable of 'extrasensory' perceptions. Strictly controlled experiments also demonstrated the direct influence of consciousness on material systems and processes independently of the human body. The true nature of this connection remains an inexplicable mystery, yet continues to have enormous appeal. Since ancient times, people have experienced this as an intuitive *certainty*, and the scientific findings that support it are now welcomed wholeheartedly.

However intangible and hidden this mystery may be, to be able to talk about it we need words and concepts that represent it. Over the course of human history, symbols and images have frequently been used to express ideas about the divine and mysterious that are difficult to put into words. Whether these are names, images, or symbols from various religious traditions or from nature, they all served to express human life in the presence of the life mystery in all its complexity: in devotion, anger, wisdom, or despair. Over the past few years I have asked myself this question: what are the symbols and images that point to life's mystery in our time?

Our thinking can't exist without images. Our language uses images that refer to the tangible reality — the reality as we experience it. To summon up images that show some of the mysterious entanglement involving consciousness and the physical reality, I have used techniques and methods from modern science, including quantum physics, psychic research, and molecular biology. I entitled the resulting artworks, which were attempts to represent the connectedness of mind and material manifestion, the '*Mind over Matter Series.*'

When I showed these series for the first time during a modest exposition in The Hague, I had no idea there was such a need to connect a spiritual experience with modern insights of science by means of images. Since then people have regularly asked me for a book containing my art works and to explain the underlying ideas. Although I have tried to put this into writing, it is difficult to talk about the great unknowing, which in fact is the basis of my study of consciousness.

While I was writing these texts it became clear to me that my work could not exist apart from a dialogue with others. I experience consciousness in an exchange with the physical world, but much more strongly in exchange with others. That is why I decided that a book about my work should consist of conversations with people with whom I have cooperated, or who I met as a result of my work. Those conversations demonstrate that there are many ways of approaching questions about consciousness and material reality. However different the approaches are, a mysterious connection between our consciousness and the world we live in emerges from each of these conversations. The deeper we try to penetrate all of this, the greater the mystery seems to become. It may be possible to approach it, but in the end words and images fail us. Yet, even if this is the case, on approaching it we experience a certain presence, something that can't be named. Exactly what Tat says after all his father's lectures:

> I understand, Father, I understand: that which can't be expressed in words, that is God!

Iebele Abel,
The Hague, August 2012

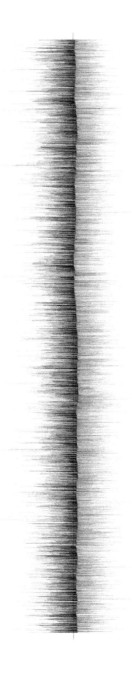

Trying to keep the line at the right side

From the series Mind over Matter (2008)
Psychokinesis experiment #1, 10th sample
Giclée print on dibond, 37 × 100 cm

Technology and Spirituality

Conversation with Peter van Kan
The Hague, October 2008

Peter van Kan is editor, meditation teacher, and musician. This chapter is an adaption of an interview taken just after the first public show of the series Mind over Matter.

Peter: You use technology in your work to create images. Why do you use technology in your work to express something spiritual?

Iebele: A small, very young beetle walked over my hand this afternoon. The insect was almost translucent; I think it had just come out of the egg. That tiny being tried bravely to discover the world of my hand all by itself. The longer one looks at such an insect, the more miraculous and mysterious its existence becomes. One may look at it in different ways, of course. One can study how its body works by looking at the metabolism, the chemical management, and the mechanical structure of its body. That is a way to get to know the phenomenon 'beetle' better. Another way to look at an insect like that is to ask oneself how its life started, why it will try to reproduce itself, and why it will die one day. The first way of looking has been developed to a high degree in our time. We live in a relatively advanced technological environment, and we are reasonably able to mold physical reality to our wishes. Even if we are highly developed in this respect, the questions the second view raise can't be answered. There are no answers to the questions about the origin and purpose of life, at least not that I know of. In spite of this, people have always asked these questions. We are aware *of* our existence, but we don't really know *who* we are. We know the phenomena, but their cause, their deepest, original cause, we don't know. We don't even know *why* a stone exists. On a more metaphysical level, we don't know the origin of our thinking either. We don't know why we know, or rather why we don't know. In this big 'not-knowing,' one can think up all kinds of explanations. A reasonably consistent idea in history is that reality has come forth from the spirit. The mind existed before matter in this view. In addition to this 'spiritual' representation, a materialistic, causal model was developed, which says that consciousness stems from matter, our bodies — in particular, from our brains. There are roughly two schools of thought. The first one says: I have a body because I think, and the other one says: I think because I have a body. The spiritual and the materialistic models differ widely from each other, mainly because the perspective is so different. The spiritual view asks for the *meaning* of phenomena; the materialistic view asks for the *explanation* of phenomena. I am interested in both perspectives because, in matter as well as in consciousness, there may be a common, universal aspect that we presume exists, even though we don't know for sure. If this presumption is right, matter as well as consciousness have 'something' which connects them with each other. My art attempts to express this common 'something.' The only way I can do this is by using the materialistic as well as the spiritual perspective in my work.

Peter: Your way of working reminds me of EEG research and biofeedback. I know computer games that work with those. Do you make your art work in the same way?

Iebele: No. I used those techniques in the past, but the techniques I work with now are different. Let me tell you something about bio- and neurofeedback first; that will make it easier to explain later what I'm doing now. I think everyone knows the heart check-up machines in hospitals. They show on a screen the heartbeat as a pulsating wave. Apparently, at the moment someone can hear or see his heartbeat, by directing his consciousness to it, he is better able to increase or decrease the heartbeat. This principle is called biofeedback. One gives feedback about the measured values to the patient or the experimental subject and, through that feedback, he becomes aware of what is happening in his body. If you are aware of something, you are better able to change these processes yourself. In the same way, you can also visualize and influence brain activity. Brain signals are much more complex than those generated by the heart, which is why in neurofeedback the signal is often fed back in a simplified way. If an animation figure moves to the left, for example, one is in a quiet mood, and if the figure moves to the right that is a signal that one's mood is getting more restless. By means of feedback in such a simplified way, one can train certain parts of the brain to become quieter or more active. Years ago, I used a similar method in a musical composition in which I produced variations in music instead of making figures move. The result of this music installation was that one reached a quiet, meditative mood.

Peter: That was in 2004, when you did a performance based on EEG and neurofeedback in a large park. You had cables attached to your head then. Now you work with a different technique that enables you to do something similar without those cables. You are no longer in physical contact with machinery and yet those machines bring forth art works, the form of which is influenced by your consciousness. Now I, and probably everyone else, would like to know what that technique is and how it works.

Iebele: Since the invention of the EEG and ECG, we have become familiar with the idea that changing moods, thoughts, and activities also lead to different brain waves and a different heartbeat. I think that has made us think in terms of consciousness more than before, but our consciousness is much more than the electrical signals of our brain activity, of course. Consciousness is about feeling, sensing, seeing things, longing for things, and so on. And even more important: we are conscious of other people and animals. We sense the feelings and emotions of others, sometimes even without seeing them. In some way or another, we are able to pick up information from our environment. We don't just do that with our senses; we also pick up more intuitive stimuli, that sometimes seem to be unrelated to sensory stimuli. Nobody knows how this kind of extrasensory perceptions works. It is a mysterious phenomenon, but it is a phenomenon we are *aware* of. We know it whenever we long for something, dream, are fearful, feel, intuit, or sense something in advance. All of this happens inside of us, and at the same time we can perceive it as a reality outside of the reality we perceive with our senses. Something magical is happening here, because even if this inner perception is immaterial — after all, we can't hold it in our hands — our inner experience really does seem to be connected with the physical reality. Joseph Banks Rhine researched extrasensory perceptions in the 1930s by asking subjects to guess cards. There were five kinds of cards, and the odds that a subject would make the right guess was 20 percent. Most subjects guessed right considerably more than 20 percent of the time. Rhine set a trend in parapsychological research with this experiment. How can you explain that people's chance of guessing the correct card from a series was above average? Are we aware of more than we perceive via our senses?

Even if it is still regarded skeptically by many mainstream scientists, the methods used in parapsychological research have improved considerably in the past eighty years. Instead of cards, we nowadays use electronic random event generators, or REGs, which are able to produce hundreds of thousands of events per second. Extensive research with these 'electronic dice' indicates that people are able to guess, to a certain extent, what the outcome will be. We are talking about marginal effects here, but they *are* present. Obviously our consciousness doesn't only work via our senses; there are other telepathic 'receivers' involved. To make it even more magical, research demonstrated the possibility of *influencing* the outcome of such electronic dice by means of intention. Guessing the outcome of sets of cards or electronic dice is called *precognition*. The term for influencing the outcome is *psychokinesis*, or making something move by non-physical means. Psychokinesis and precognition are similar to each other in several ways, but for both it is a question of a not-yet-understood relationship between spirit and matter.

Peter: To study this phenomenon further and to use it in your art works, you have cooperated with Dick Bierman, professor of Exceptional Experiences at the University of Amsterdam.

Iebele: Dick Bierman is also a physicist. I asked him to help me make a system that would enable me to transfer psychokinetic phenomena into image and music. Until then I had only read about psychokinesis in popular scientific literature. I wanted to find out if the experiments described there really worked; I wanted to do them personally and experience it for myself. If it is true that the mind can influence things and machines, it should also be possible to make art using one's inner experience, directly from inspiration. What fascinated me most of all — and this is a major difference from the EEG computer games you mentioned — is that if one investigates psychokinesis using REGs, one doesn't need wires or cables on one's head or fingers. With REGs, one literally studies the possible correlation between immaterial mind and material reality. The correlation between those two can't be expressed by recognized physical variables like power, voltage, or an electromagnetic field. Nevertheless, Dick explained to me, step by step, how to express that correlation. He showed me the way in a field which I never thought would interest me: the calculation of probability. Essentially, an REG is like some kind of dice and you want to know whether your consciousness corresponds in one way or another with such a machine. You figure out what the *chance* is of a certain result from such a machine being related to your consciousness. Chance is of course hardly a descriptive variable for consciousness, but it is rather interesting that consciousness is able to influence chance in the case of an outcome for 'electronic dice.' It took me a while to understand that chance clearly is the only way up till now to prove scientifically that our consciousness and our physical reality may influence each other or not.

Peter: That sounds scientific, but you are an artist. What matters to you is, whether you are able to show by image or sound that consciousness has an influence on our reality.

Iebele: The chance factor in my work may not sound very artistic, but it is important. We experience the coinciding of a conscious thought and a corresponding event as special. In terms of coincidence, the chance is very small that your mother will call at the moment you think about her. The chance is so tiny, that, when it does happen, you are inclined to ascribe a special meaning to it. You say for example that you and your mother are 'connected with each other in spirit' at that moment or you call it telepathy. In the past, people probably attached more significance to such seemingly chance happenings. Magical thinking starts from interconnectedness and applies this principle in a practical way. Thinking in terms of interconnectedness still exists, but in our time it has retreated into the background because coincidence now can apparently be explained in terms of cause and effect. In chemistry, mathematics, and physics, and even in neurology and biology, coincidences and chaotic processes are often treated as deterministic, that is, as the result of a series of causal processes. According to this line of thinking, free will can't exist because our universe is supposed to be rational, causal. There is no place in this causal universe for something as indeterminate as free will. The Darwinist idea about evolution starts from causal chaotic processes, in which consciousness hardly plays any role: new biological varieties have their origin in random mutations, and if such a coincidental creature is successful in surviving, its genes are passed on to its offspring. But suppose — and this is an idea that has existed for thousands of years in mysticism, science, and philosophy — the processes in nature and in our consciousness are less causal than they seem? If we assume that *a*, or *our*, or *my* consciousness is an active part of the processes in our bodies and in the world, then we are less at the mercy of random chance than we might think. What I wanted to study is whether I really could influence a random process by conscious intention. I suspected that an increased inspiration could not only lead to creative inner processes, but also to special deviations of chance outcomes in physical reality. The work 'Deviation from a Standard Distribution' is a good example of this. The pebbles in this work come from a computer database. Every boulder has been photographed and downloaded to a computer. During this experiment — almost all my works are in fact experiments — a boulder was selected at random 200 times per second and placed in circles, also at random, on the sheet of paper. The inner circle in this image is a textbook example of a normal distribution. If you empty a pail of pebbles you will get a pattern like that. You can more or less predict this pattern using the theory of probability. In the case of this work, an REG serves as electronic 'dice' and determined the pattern the boulders fell in. Theoretically, an REG produces ideal randomness, and functions according to a mathematical model of a normal random distribution. At the beginning of the experiment, the boulders 'dropped' in a pile on top of each other, exactly as expected. The thought test during this experiment was for the boulders to deviate from this pattern, in such a way as to create an extra circle outside the normal distribution.

Peter: You wanted this outer circle to appear, and it happened merely by your *wanting* it. That is the spiritual element of your work; you show that consciousness has an effect in the world.

Iebele: Apart from all the technology and theory, the works in the series *Mind over Matter* have a mysterious beauty; that is the artistic value. The images originated at moments when I was particularly inspired, and that can be seen. *That* is what amazes me. There is an order pointing to synchronicity, but synchronicity with what? A universal order seems to exist in the world, something present in everything. Such an image reflects some of this order, at least that is what I see in it. But I couldn't have made it like this 'myself.' Not by hand, I mean, but I was able to do it by *mind*.

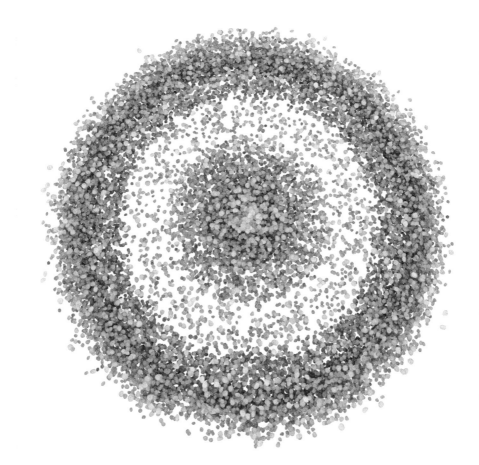

Deviation from a standard distribution (River boulders)

From the series Mind over Matter (2008)
Psychokinesis experiment #8, 3rd sample (p = 0.0095)
Giclée print on dibond, 112 × 112 cm

Peter: How do you prepare for making an artwork by means of an REG?

Iebele: When I started to investigate this method I thought the best results would be obtained in a meditative state, but in the end all the art works were created right after setting up an experiment. That is logical too when looking back, because at the moment all the technical preparations have been done, one likes to know if everything is working. For every work I collected stones, leaves, and straws. I turned that collecting work into fun excursions. In the studio, these materials were photographed; a job that needs one's full attention. Each experiment needed software preparations as well, which led me step by step to a new experiment. At a certain moment, all the preparations had been done and I could start the experiment by sitting down, concentrating my thoughts, and pushing a button. Within five to ten minutes, an artwork was created, purely by my thinking strongly of the result I wanted to reach.

Peter: During that time you don't do anything but concentrate. You don't touch anything; the only contact between you and your machines is your consciousness.

Iebele: Yes, that is what is so fascinating. You called it contact, but it is really a mystery to me as to what exactly is happening. Is it contact? Is it influence? Is it synchronicity? The first few experiments I did were always successful, again and again. They resulted in what I expected. If I repeated the same experiment later when, for example, someone came to visit, that strong result was hardly there at all. I think that is extraordinary. Obviously my inspiration plays a role in producing such a work. And the preparations seem to play a role, too. Inspiration and preparation are apparently important for getting these results.

Peter: That reminds me of top-class sport. I interviewed Gerard Nijboer, who was the Netherlands' best marathon runner in the 1980s. I also talked on one occasion to skating coach Gerard Kemkers about record performances and top form. What you do resembles top sport, because you have to peak in your work. To peak, you need preparation. You work towards that single moment. One sees that in big tournaments. And later, if people try to get the same score again, the tension is gone and the result is less too.

Iebele: I think such a comparison is a good one. I talked about this with Dick Bierman a lot as well. He too said there seems to be a connection between the preparation, the quantity of energy one puts into that, and the result. I like the example of a musician. Learning to play an instrument requires years of training. When a musician practices for a performance, he still makes all kinds of mistakes. The moment he steps on to the platform, he is able to perform a piece of music almost flawlessly. The body, the consciousness, the notes, and the instrument seem to be one. At such a moment, a sort of magic comes into being between him and the public. The musician seems to develop wings. There is contact between the musician, the music, and the public. All the preparations come together during the performance. If music is played with 'wings,' it resembles a mystical experience, because people strongly experience connectedness. It was like that when I made the series *Mind over Matter*. When I talk about it, it sometimes sounds very theoretical or technical, but it is ultimately about reaching a moment of heightened inspiration. Technology serves the goal of reaching that moment *and* recording it. Compare this with the technique a painter, a musician, or a sportsman needs to master in order to achieve something excellent. I use technique in the same way. It is true that I have developed the technique I use myself, because it did not exist yet. That's how I have to handle it; just like a painter, who mixes his own paint, knows very well what his paint can and can't do. By doing all of this myself, the preparation time is longer, and that probably influences the result. I once heard about a racing cyclist who designed the wheels and pedals of his own bike, to get better results. I recognize such an attitude. When I was still painting, I preferred to make my own paint, as that is the best way to be in touch with your material, and I still try to make everything myself. My technical jargon therefore is sometimes a little detailed and inaccessible, but I nevertheless try to explain how I make my work because the idea behind it is part of its meaning. I hope people find that just as interesting as when a soccer player talks about his shoe laces. There is another link with top-class sport: it takes up one's daily life completely. Everything revolves around that one result. It is not so surprising, in fact, that good results are produced from time to time. That is the aim of the work, and at a certain moment everything seems to fall into place. Everything you have put into it comes out. That is also an emotional moment. I can be exhausted afterwards, empty in a certain way. Indeed, it's just like sport, although I am not really a sporting type myself.

Peter: A sporting achievement is very concrete. The score is 1-0, or one is the fastest marathon runner. It is visible and measurable. The results in art are much less tangible. You use maybe the least tangible aspect of art, the inspiration, as a starting point for your work. Is that the reason why you are looking for dialogue with disciplines outside art, to get a grip on something that is barely tangible?

Iebele: Expressing the immaterial — like our consciousness, for example — by making concrete, tangible art works and music invites dialogue. Dialogue is one way to reach a better understanding of the subjects we are talking about. In my work I use questions, hypotheses, and insights from the progressive sciences (biophysics, quantum physics and psychic research) with the same goal: to learn to understand better. I also use the technology, methods, and concepts of these sciences. Concepts like coherence, potency, entropy, chaos and order, energy and information are variables that can describe interconnectivity and consciousness. I have talked with many researchers in the past few years about these concepts, for example at Princeton University, where they did a lot of consciousness research. It seems to be true that when we want to comprehend our consciousness and life's mystery, we have no choice but to restore the importance of the subjective experience. The old model that strives for objectivity seems to exclude many observations in order to remain valid. Looked at from this point of view, cooperation between science and art is important, because they are able to complement each other mutually. Art's contribution is that it has a tradition in which subjective experience has always played a role.

Peter: You often talk about the limitations of the technological-scientific model for the development of our consciousness, but isn't it true that our consciousness has evolved enormously, just because of the technological developments?

Iebele: Certainly, I think we may be grateful to technology and above all to science for the insights they have brought forth and will bring forth in the process of our development. What I'd like to emphasize is that the model from which our technological society arose has become so exclusive that we need to contemplate how we can widen our model of reality in this time. I think it is important to emphasize that the latest developments in science seem to connect more and more with the old traditions of wisdom like esoterics and mysticism. If we really find confirmation for the idea that everything in our universe is interconnected, and that everything in our physical reality arose from 'mind,' from consciousness, that will have an enormous impact on our development.

Peter: Are you also saying that the reality we perceive now, in this sidewalk café, may be an illusion, a construction of our consciousness?

Iebele: Even though things around us may have a physical reality, we know this reality as such only because we tune our communal perception to it. By reaching a certain agreement about the use of descriptions and metaphors we are able to describe physical reality and share our perceptions. At the same time, the consensus about our reality is a filter limiting the scope of perception. As soon as I tell you about things which I can see or hear, but which aren't perceptible for you, we find ourselves in an area that is called subjective. The scientific method avoids all subjectivity and accepts only those perceptions which can be reproduced, preferably by people who are independent of each other. This method has strongly influenced our perception and it degenerated into a doctrine that labels perceptions which are not reproducible or testable as 'not true.' Seen from the perspective of possibilities given to us by our consciousness, it does not seem right to me to doubt any perceptions. Every perception in my opinion is a product of our consciousness. Maybe our reality feels so dense, in the sense that this table here feels solid, because we have developed the metaphors and descriptions of a physical reality so strongly over thousands, maybe tens of thousands of years. As soon as our consciousness leaves this dense reality, however — for example, during our dreams — our reality is suddenly much more pliable. We then enter a world where we still have visual, auditory, and sensory perceptions, but in a much more flexible form. We don't recognize this fluid reality only from our dreams; our whole imagination has this flexibility. We are very well able to imagine our plans or our longings. Then we try to realize those plans within the powerful limits that daily reality apparently draws up for us. The question, however, is whether the limitations we experience in our physical reality are the product of the way we describe them ourselves; in other words, whether our physical life and the slowness we experience every day in our development, are indeed determined by the laws of physical mechanics. This question is interesting because natural laws do not always seem to hold true, or in any case, to apply in a linear way in time. Our consciousness, for example, appears to be non-linear; it is able simply to exchange time and place and is, as such, maybe a non-local phenomenon, as found in quantum mechanics. If the classical mechanistic view doesn't apply to the way our consciousness works, maybe we shouldn't try to explain it from this model. We may need a much broader model to encompass all our experiences. A new term 'science of the subjective' has recently been coined, with the aim to emancipate the individual subjective perception into the business of the exact sciences. Art can benefit from that too; it is especially art, after all, that allows room for describing both internal and external experiences subjectively.

Peter: In your series *Mind over Matter*, you used psychokinesis to study the relationship between consciousness and matter in an almost scientific way. You dropped leaves and pebbles in a special pattern, exclusively by using the power of thinking, of your intentions. Is what you make art or science? In my opinion it is art, but how do you see that yourself?

Iebele: My work is *not* science, not in the strict sense of the word. When I studied at art academy, I was nineteen at the time; I worked with themes taken from mysticism and esoterics. At that time, my fascination for the spiritual dimensions wasn't well understood, especially because there was a lot of resistance to the dogmas of ecclesiastical thinking. The discussion in art avoided spirituality; at least, that was true for the artistic environment I hung around in. For a major part of my career as an artist, I have tried to find ways, within the domain of art, to raise subjects like that for dialogue. Over the last few decades, new insights into the relationship between consciousness and our physical reality have caused an enormous social movement which has once more found inspiration in the esoteric idea that consciousness precedes material manifestation. This movement has hardly found any place in modern artistic discourse. That is the main reason I made these works; maybe that's why they have been received enthusiastically. Of course the subject is ideal for creating a variety of different expression forms. The way I do it is only one of them. You can see the series *Mind over Matter* as intention experiments, expressed in figurative work. During these experiments, by working with intentions I specifically started out from my own will. The methods I had developed made it possible that an artwork came into being without my having any physical contact with the machines that actually brought forth the product. You can regard these works as frozen moments of heightened inspiration. I look for a way to express the immaterial qualities of my consciousness. That fits in better with the tradition of mysticism and art than with the tradition of science.

Peter: Of course, having a bridge with science makes your story more convincing.

Iebele: I don't know about that. What I do is very debatable from a scientific point of view, because the way I work is first and foremost artistic.

Peter: Why is it debatable? Because you are always your own subject in your work? Because you don't do double-blind research?

Iebele: Yes, exactly. I don't produce any proof for things in my work; that's not what I'm after. And there isn't — and I wouldn't want it either — any inspection of the way I work. There are no video cameras present while I'm making something, and therefore you can't check if I'm cheating. I make my work in my studio, in my own intimate, magical circle; that's where it all happens. Very simply said, my work is all about observing my own consciousness. How can I show the observation that I am a conscious being? That is the question I ask, and more specifically: am I connected with other conscious beings or with matter? And if that is true, how? And what does this mean?

Peter: Isn't it possible to have a group of, say, fifty people in a room for a whole day? To work all day long on mutual solidarity and then to do an experiment?

Iebele: I wanted to try that at first, too. In the series *Mind over Matter* I investigated whether it was possible to influence a certain process by directing my conscious attention. That appeared to be possible to a certain extent. Something happened. But I continued to think while doing the experiments — and the thought became stronger as I progressed — that 'wanting to influence' is not my primary intention.

The thought that consciousness influences reality is working in two directions, I think. The most beautiful experiences in my life are not that something happened the way I wanted; to the contrary. The most beautiful experiences are when I received something or was allowed to give something. In my current work I study what happens when I witness processes, mind-matter events. I can use the same method I've already developed, but I'm using it in a different way. I'm not going to investigate the element 'will' or 'intention' any further for a while. Now, I direct myself to 'receiving' and 'perceiving.' That's why I have developed a machine that produces music solely by listening to it. This instrument can be active during a show or lecture, and people can experience for themselves how this music corresponds harmoniously and interacts with the feelings they experience. The working of this instrument is not based on intentions, but its aim is to arouse a sense of connectedness.[1] During the presentation of this instrument, I ask the public to be observers and be receptive to what the music evokes. That is quite a different attitude from *wanting* something. The experience I have with this music so far is that people like to listen to it. The music seems to produce a heightened sense of connectedness.

Peter: I see a staggering number of possibilities and applications for this principle. You could see it as the beginning of the realization that we are creating continuously. Once this hurdle has been taken and assumed to be true, a door will open to a whole new world.

Iebele: Multinational Motorola once commissioned Dean Radin to design a 'mind switch.' A switch that would turn on or off when someone wanted it. They were looking for a finger print in the mind pattern, based on random event generators, so that a switch like that could recognize from whom the thought was coming. That failed, but the idea was that such a 'mind switch' need not work locally, limited by time or space. In other words, someone could turn it on or off from a distance, purely because that person wanted it. Something like that resembles science fiction, but obviously it is being taken so seriously that a big multinational has put money into it. Anyway, I don't think the most important applications will be in the area of control. I think

---

1 This system has been extensively improved after the first publication of this book in 2009. In September 2012 the system was introduced as "Indeterminate Synthetic Music Feedback" (ISMF) for therapeutic intervention, during the international "Consciousness in Crisis" conference in The Netherlands.

we will realize more and more that our consciousness plays a role in the way thoughts and feelings become tangible in our world. Even if we don't understand exactly how, consciousness and physical reality have something to do with each other. New words and images will probably develop, describing our consciousness like a living, active entity that matters in our life. As long as our consciousness cannot be expressed concretely, 'thinking' that consciousness can lead to change in the world is a *belief*. I think it is important to reach consensus about what *living consciousness* is. It isn't easy to reach a consensus about what consciousness is, because the most important characteristic of consciousness seems to be that it is just a little different for each person. So we are looking for objectification of something that is experienced subjectively. That seems to be contradictory, but it should be possible. It is like religion. There is common ground in all religions. If you look for the similarities, you can talk without any problem with people from different religious backgrounds.

Peter: That has caused enough misery already; believing in something without seeing the similarity with other convictions, and then repeatedly clashing with people who believe something else.

Iebele: It is the same with consciousness. There are people who *believe* that consciousness has creative powers. It may be true. We know in any case that we are conscious beings, but each one of us is conscious in a different way. What is the common factor? It is a factor that surpasses belief. The exciting thing is, of course, that all of us live together in a system in which everyone has certain longings and puts forward various ideas, in whatever way. People often say: "You can direct your life by means of intentions." I don't want to contradict this, but I do think it is important to realize that we live on a planet with very many *different* living beings, all of whom have their own dreams, longings, and intentions. Your individual power functions within that whole. I think what matters is learning to think in terms of "What do we want to reach together?" instead of "What do I want badly?" If the image of a collective longing becomes more and more clear, it will be easier to create or experience it.

Peter: Do you think that the world will eventually improve if that happens?
Iebele: In the end it is a personal process, of course. There's no way

you can force someone else into such a process because everyone is different, with his own point of departure and his own continuation process. What you can try is to keep the common denominators as widely based as possible, so that you leave as much space as possible in your thinking for many different lines of approach and from different people. Consciousness is such a denominator for me. It is a broad concept that wouldn't have a meaning if many people didn't presume it to have a certain power. We perceive with our consciousness. Everyone seems to agree on that. In addition to that, there is a notion that our consciousness is creative and thus creating. This ability to create has been mentioned for a very long time in mystic and esoteric literature and this 'knowledge' has been getting more popular in recent years. The question is, whether our consciousness' creative ability can produce a certain result in the world without physically doing something. That is an important question, because if we know it to be true, we will probably use our consciousness differently. The world could improve in that way, but it could also become much worse as well. It depends on what someone wants to do with such knowledge. I make images and music with it.

Words and Images

Conversation with Tijn Touber
Amsterdam, November 2008

For many years Tijn Touber was editor of Ode Magazine *and writer of a variety of books about enlightment. For his research Tijn Touber has interviewed tens, if not hundreds of people who have — each in their own way — contributed to the idea that enlightenment can be within everyone's reach.*

Tijn: In your art and specifically in the series *Mind over Matter* you tried to give shape to the ancient idea that consciousness is the origin of matter. You want to tell an old story anew, using a modern technology. How did you get the idea to do this?

Iebele: Years before I started this project, I read about research into deviations in the behaviour of random event generators that were correlated with human consciousness. Popular literature associates the idea that it is possible to influence a machine, a material thing — a black box — by consciousness, with the way our intentions and longings can determine our personal life. The bestseller *The Secret* and the movie *What the Bleep Do We Know* suggest, for example, that the relationship between consciousness and matter has been proven scientifically. If this is true, we could take advantage of this knowledge in the sense that we could create our own world, purely by the way in which we think. This thought is inspiring, but I presumed the complexity of our existence is not as easy to interpret as that. That's why I started to read a number of scientific studies around this theme. I was curious about scientific research and the conclusions of the researchers themselves. I found these studies more convincing than the publications written for the general public, mainly because the conclusions of these researchers were less certain than the popular reading matter had led us to suppose. This is because scientific research evokes many expectations, but also many reservations and questions, especially among the researchers themselves. I connect

Mind over Matter with the saying by Hermes Trismegistus: "as above, so below." I was curious if the insights from traditional wisdom would indeed be confirmed by modern scientific methods or if this could be expressed in art. But suppose there is no correlation between consciousness and what happens at a physical level after all, and all assumptions in this area turn out to be wrong? The complexity I see is that, on the one hand, there is a longing for a world that works the way you like it and, on the other hand, there is a factual world that shapes or doesn't shape or only partially shapes itself around your longings. I think there are a lot of people who wish or 'sense' intuitively that the physical reality is a product of our consciousness. Sound evidence for this is still missing. Thus, the idea exists only in the imagination, even if it has already stood firm as a metaphysical concept for thousands of years.

Tijn: In spite of this, consciousness clearly has an immediate influence. If I have a sexual thought, my physical being is influenced; I can see that in my body. Sound evidence is not really needed to prove that consciousness influences matter.

Iebele: On that level, our thoughts manifest themselves very clearly of course. It seems to be self-evident that our body reacts to our thoughts, but it still is a mystery how that works exactly. Throughout history, new discoveries have often been used to explain inexplicable phenomena. Think about the discovery of the electromagnetic field, for example. Shortly after this discovery was made, this field was held responsible, albeit hypothetically, for quite a range of phenomena, like telepathy and faith healing. Apparently, a discovery and its various practical applications generates a certain amount of enthusiasm for approaching life's mystery anew. I think that is interesting because, despite our relative ignorance, one single insight obviously evokes particularly far horizons in our imagination. One new discovery may thus explain the whole creation in a model that, as a result of pure and sincere enthusiasm, the imagination can comprehend. This occurs especially in the popular interpretation of new scientific insights. It happened for example with quantum physics, relativity theory, chaos theory, the hypothesis of a morphogenetic field, and the theory on biophotons, which are all trendy at this moment in time. Again and again there is excitement, hope that we will be able to understand the entire universe one day. Such euphoria evaporates when new, contradictory insights are offered, but as soon as a new model is suggested, our image of reality changes for an extended period because the new images and metaphors have to be inserted into the description of reality. A theory doesn't have to be right or verifiable, by any means, to have a tremendous influence on our perception. To get back to the sexual excitement you just mentioned: its physical expression is clear. Nevertheless, this observation may be less self-evident than you think. Someone told me once that one day it was *discovered* you could hear your own heart beat. Were people previously unable to hear their own hearts or to even feel them? Could it be that people in a distant past didn't notice that their bodies changed when they made love?

Tijn: What you are saying is actually that our reality, or the perception thereof, is formed by using metaphors, models, and descriptions. A recent metaphor is to compare our brain to the way computers work. This way, we are better able to understand how the brain works. We don't understand the brain, but we do understand how computers work. They have memories, they can produce images and sounds, and they can make logical connections. Maybe 'quantum physics' has become a certain metaphor too, a way of thinking we use to try and explain reality.

Iebele: The tricky thing is that we know a metaphor isn't always true. The computer as a metaphor for our brain falls short in important aspects. The main shortcoming of this metaphor in my opinion is that a machine essentially differs from an organism or an organ. By using machines as metaphors for living systems, one in fact limits the view of life. Metaphors like that may estrange us from the living beings we are. I may be taking things rather far here, but I can imagine that inaccurate metaphors may unsettle society, and individuals as well. Once this is understood, new metaphors that may function better, will perhaps replace the old ones. Quantum physics is often used nowadays as a metaphor in all kinds of holistic ideas because, for many people, the purely materialistic model is no longer usable. The vision behind the holistic idea, however, is wider than any physical theory. Perhaps because of all the advances, especially the many technological applications, we have started using metaphors from science and technology to describe phenomena which still evoke substantial questions within the scientific community itself. Looking for images and descriptions that fit our time is no small matter in my opinion either.

Tijn: Do you look for the final answer to this kind of questions in your work, or does it suffice to play with these themes as an artist?

Iebele: Today's view of life in fact provokes a conflict because of the model with a spiritual self and a material body; that is how I experience it. This is an old model, a dualistic one. However, a satisfying physical model, reflecting the modern longing for unity, simply does not exist. At least, not that I know of. Nevertheless, I presume there is an order, a coherence in the overwhelming complexity of this world. Somewhere I think there is an intelligence holding all of it together, making it the way it is. I exist in this reality too, both in the form of a relatively stable body and in a continuously changing consciousness of it. Body and mind seem to get together in that one reality of perception. The statement "I'm aware of my body and consciousness" expresses what I mean; it represents an important value for me, because everything I see and hear has a self-evidence that is undeniable. What I perceive corresponds exactly with my consciousness of it; only in language is one thing distinguished from the other by becoming two separate constructs. Maybe that's why I feel so connected with language, descriptions, and models. That can keep me busy year after year: how I can fit my perceptions and experiences into the physical context of the world in which I live, the things and processes of which I am a part.

Tijn: Perceiving is actually assuming something you perceive to be true.

Iebele: Exactly. As an observer, you yourself are the channel to reality. Pure perception is healing, I think, because it brings us back to ourselves, beyond all the abstract models and layers that we have fabricated to explain all kinds of things.

Tijn: Do you intend to stretch your perception, too? Or is it just the opposite: bringing it back to yourself, to nothingness, so to speak. After all, in nothingness you lose all your concepts. You can make two movements: inward and outward.

Iebele: I find both movements interesting, for in both you can try to widen the limits. In one's external relationships, for example, with people, as well as in the internally directed relationship with oneself, one continually meets 'blocks' that disappear if one's ideas are given more freedom. If you accept something — thoughts, perceptions, other people, or yourself — as they are, you actually broaden your own perception. Acceptance in that sense is getting rid of a concept.

Tijn: Your bandwidth is stretched. You experience more because you exclude less.

Iebele: Yes, and that produces a certain modesty, because in that process you notice that every stretch broadens the experience, and that it can expand into what you could call a cosmic experience. But I have to say that such an experience, with me at least, is rare and doesn't last very long. Talking and reading about such an experience may bring one closer to it. That works best when nothing explicit is said, when nothing specific is pointed out. Great teachers know how to indicate a direction without telling you exactly where you could go. Imagination takes over, and in the space of imagination you can arrive at the place you really want to be. This place itself seems to be unnamable; words and images always fall short.

Tijn: That is what I like about art and that is what I think you are able to offer, because art leaves a lot of space. That is a space in particular where the public can give their own interpretation. The artist inspires people to enter a certain area to be sure, but the people themselves actually step into it. In this way, space is offered so we can investigate other dimensions.

Iebele: Art work *expresses* a perception *in a certain way*, by taking a certain perspective. In my work I try to bring this perspective outside the strictly sensory. What moves me to make things is that the exchange of experiences continuously raises new questions and all these questions cause a certain inner unrest. I mean here the common questions people often ask themselves: "Why am I here? What am I doing here? What am I seeing here? What am I hearing? Why do I feel love? Why do I feel anger? Why do I feel fear? Why do I feel safe?" Luckily there are quite a variety of ways to deal with these questions. I chose to use my work to direct attention to generating harmony and inner quietness, because those are the aspects in life I find most comforting myself. At the same time, I try to understand — to penetrate more deeply into — what causes confusion and restlessness. I try to organize what I see and what I feel. I think the trickiest thing is the separation between my longings and what there is. I try to remove that separation by using new thoughts, new 'models,' but the paradoxical thing is that they still are thoughts, that don't necessarily come from the perception of something that really exists. That's why I make things: obviously I so badly want the things in the world to be the way I long them to be, that I start making them myself. But the things I make do not reflect my perceptions, they are *thoughts*. Complex thoughts that I transfer into images, music, and words on paper. I hope to design those thoughts in such a way that other people recognize themselves in them. If recognition happens, it gives me peace of mind. The world appears to be inhabited by people who have more or less the same thoughts, or become inspired by such thoughts. I am not alone then.

Tijn: You not only make thoughts. You make images and music too. Thoughts by themselves are obviously not enough for you.

Iebele: Making images and music gives me satisfaction, because it is tangible work. For me, making an image means elaborating a thought, but without words.

Tijn: In this way, I think your work has space and quietness, because words are not needed any more.

Iebele: I hope so; I really do. Someone once said about my work that he thought it was clean, in the sense of 'not dirty.' I thought that was a beautiful compliment because that is exactly what I want to reach. You know, I can hardly believe that my work could speak for itself because I thought so much about it before I made it. I'm hardly able to see the quietness in my own work. I do see it in my music, while that too is made from thoughts, structures, and theories. But maybe I don't need to explain my work at all. Maybe I just need to make it.

Tijn: Maybe not 'just.' I think what makes it so beautiful is exactly the balance between the art work and the story behind it. I recently saw a man, David Whyte, an Irish poet. He teaches people how to permeate into a different reality by means of the word. He said that real art and poetry open up roads to realities that are narrow, scary, and thrilling. In art you look for these limits, as it were. The nice thing about his lecture was that he was explaining concepts so clearly. He was teaching us; there was a clear line in his story, but we didn't realize it because it was beautifully interspersed with poems that touched the public very deeply; I could really feel it. He recited the lines by heart, somehow opening up our minds to the next piece of information. I listened to him breathlessly for twelve hours on end, and yet he never became boring because he continually alternated between head and heart. Science and art. That is what you do too. People feel a certain connectedness when they see your art work in the series *Mind over Matter*, but the images indeed 'prove' very tangibly that it is possible to get a specific result by having intentions.

Iebele: One of the first experiments was wanting to make a ball on a computer screen bigger or smaller by means of 'thought power,' as I called it at the time. Dick Bierman, who was the first one to help me make art works this way, warned me that it might work the first few times but, after a while, no longer. At first I thought it strange to hear this from someone who had spent a large part of his life researching exactly what I wanted to study. Not until much later did I understand that 'beginner's luck' does indeed have a meaning. Dick wouldn't say it in so many words maybe, but beginner's luck does play a role in the way in which consciousness and the physical reality are, or appear to be, connected with each other. The way I look at it now is that, in my first series of works, beginner's luck played a role. They have not only become images with a certain artistic value, but the statistical probability that these images would arise was very low as well. This low probability one could interpret as 'proof' that in these works my intentions did indeed determine the result. During the first show, this chance value was stated on signs. The chance in these works determined the result you see; the intention experiment was that a low probability would produce the image I had in mind, while a normal chance would produce a work without a clear visible pattern. All works met these 'verifiable' criteria. What I noticed while preparing those art works was that as I approached the moment in which I could let the works come into being, my enthusiasm increased. My feeling of satisfaction and pleasure increased as I came closer to the moment when all the preparations were done. It is important to realize I had worked for over a year developing these experiments without seeing results. Software had to be written, machines had to be bought, and I had studied the theory behind psychokinesis and so on. I had also photographed the hundreds of objects I wanted to use as material for the art works. All in all, this period of preparation created an enormous expectation, and when I 'pushed the button' for the first time to make the first art work in the series happen, this first result was, in one word, magnificent. This first experiment lasted about ten minutes, and I did my utmost to influence the noise from the random event generator as strongly as possible. And that is what happened. Before my eyes, the image arose exactly the way I had expected it to, while the chance odds for this to happen was rather small. It required a tremendously strong effort to sustain my concentration and not to disturb the emerging image. It simply *had* to succeed. The euphoria I experienced in those ten minutes is almost impossible to describe. The whole project that I had worked on for over a year manifested itself in one brilliant experience. And the fact that it really happened in front of my eyes was something I had not experienced before. It was as if something within me, an expectation or a longing, happened outside me as well, in the machines. This sensation had an enormous reinforcing effect on me for several months. All of the other experiments I made in that period may have succeeded because of that. Later, I badly wanted to repeat that, of course, or have other people experience it. Sometimes it works, sometimes it doesn't. The magic seems to disappear. That is why the whole happening is so special and, above all, so valuable; one doesn't have any control over it. Dick Bierman was right: beginner's luck, but then as a very tangible phenomenon and with an enormous added value.

Tijn: You used the word expectation. That is a beautiful word. It may be the key to the moment you wanted to reach. The funny thing is that it stops working as soon as you start expecting the expectation to work. But how does it work?

Iebele: I don't know. I wish I did.

Tijn: Is it possible that if you aren't full of expectations in the sense of 'I'm curious to know what is going to happen' but more like 'that must happen again,' you have already created a picture instead of letting the miracle happen? You know what I noticed? Where spiritual development is concerned, the development process has much less to do with directing, than with receiving. One is more effective when receiving than when steering.

Iebele: What you call 'receiving,' is getting close to a religious process that, in more traditional terms, one could call a form of surrender to God. Maybe that is an even deeper motive for becoming involved in this theme. For me, talking about God equals exploring your own ability to comprehend.

Tijn: I like that, because that way you connect the mystic-religious with the artistic and with the scientific. What touches me deeply is being full of expectation. I feel this is the real key to the question. I'm reminded of *The Secret*. That book was published in 2006 but it already seems so old fashioned. In my opinion that way of being involved in spirituality is outmoded now. The thought: 'I'm going to transmit something, because then I'll get a new job, a better wife, or a new car,' is a kind of spiritual materialism that was rather trendy for a while.

Iebele: Maybe we can see spiritual development as a process with a certain history. I'm thinking about Hans Christian Ørsted, who discovered the relationship between magnetism and electricity in 1820. He discovered this by means of an observation that seems very self-evident to us now. He saw that the magnetic compass needles moved when they were held close to a wire conveying an electric current. He was unable to explain this phenomenon but published his findings after a few years anyway. Shortly after that André-Marie Ampère was able to integrate the phenomenon in a mathematical model clarifying the relationship between magnetism and electricity. Later, James Maxwell calculated that electricity and magnetism move with the speed of light and concluded that light and magnetism were possibly similar phenomena. That is how Maxwell invented the concept 'electromagnetic field.' These discoveries have had an enormous impact on our lives. Practically all modern technology is using them. What I find interesting is that not only technology, but our spiritual body of thought as well, has been influenced by these discoveries. Spiritually developed people talk about an 'energy' they feel, or a 'radiation.' That puts one in mind of the idea of a field. The book *The Field* by Lynne McTaggart — which is often quoted as a bridge between science and spirituality — is exemplary for the popular use of the concept 'field.' In my opinion, it isn't certain if there is something like a field in the spiritual domain, the mystic-religious. Whether or not the correlations found in science between consciousness and random event generators are explainable by a field is still an open question. Possibly something quite different from a field is at work here.

Tijn: What strikes me is that you really want to understand it all. That isn't easy, because you bring several things together: art, science, and spirituality and you keep coming back to consciousness.

Iebele: Just like Örstadt took the strange behavior of compass needles seriously, we in our time are busy scrutinizing the phenomenon consciousness. It seems to me we are penetrating certain aspects of our consciousness in our time, and even though we may not quite understand them, we still see them differently from roughly a century ago. It seems we are laying new connections between consciousness and reality. We are looking for regularities, hoping to get a better grip on ourselves and our environments. It isn't at all certain that it is possible to describe our consciousness on a one-to-one basis by means of physical variables, but at a certain moment we may find a new concept: something like a 'field,' but different. Nowadays, theorists talk about 'information' and 'coherence,' for example. The 'field' concept in the context of consciousness could be exchanged for a different concept because most likely we have to think beyond the already known field concepts like 'electromagnetism' to understand our consciousness better.

Tijn: Why do you think that the field metaphor should be replaced? For most people it is a useful concept.

Iebele: The field concept was introduced by Maxwell in 1864 as part of a model in which the speed of light, and thus time too, played a role. That's where the shoe pinches for me. It is the question as to whether time plays a role in the phenomenon 'consciousness' as Lynn McTaggart describes it in *The Field*. My consciousness appears to me to be a non-local phenomenon. I mean that when I observe my consciousness — call it inner viewing — time and space don't seem to play a role any more. Actually, in the research into the relationship between consciousness and physical processes, time and place don't seem to play a role either.

Tijn: You say time may not play a role in our consciousness, but we *are* aware of time, aren't we?

Iebele: In dreamland, time doesn't play a role, but if we are awake it does. Even when we are awake, it is a very relative concept on an instinctive level. Time — and, related to that, the speed of light — may be a variable that connects our consciousness to something we experience as physical reality. A simple thought experiment or a meditation, in which you detach yourself from the time experience, has an enormous impact on the space you are able to experience in your consciousness. That's how it works for me at least. Suppose we could describe our consciousness better, for example, by leaving some variables out of our world view and, if necessary, adding new, still unknown variables. Suppose we one day get just as unequivocal a grip on the phenomena of consciousness as we now have on electromagnetic fields and other physical phenomena. That could well have a much greater impact on our society than all the other discoveries that have been made so far. I don't think this is just unbridled fantasy, for we can perceive and experience natural phenomena as well as our consciousness. After all, haven't all discoveries and insights originated from observation? I can imagine us entering an 'era of consciousness,' step by step, in which our reality eventually resembles a dream; there, everything that appears fixed and immovable will have more the character of a liquid, just like the transfer from one reality into another in dreams. Sometimes I think that is our future, but I realize, too, that all of what I'm saying now doesn't have to be true at all. These thoughts may be nothing but the wish to escape reality, escaping the realization of the possibility that there is nothing after death, not even dreams.

Tijn: You think all of it up, however, all those thoughts are a form of creativity. What you've said here is, of course, your inspiration to make your works.

Iebele: Using old-fashioned language I could call inspiration a 'holy fire.' I have always felt that fire burn in me. My problem used to be that I didn't have any point of contact to express this fire. I even noticed some hostility when I talked about it, in myself, as an inner conflict, as well as outside myself, as a confusion of tongues with people who obviously didn't know this fire, or experienced it in an entirely different way from myself. As I learnt to talk better about my inspiration — my amazement about the miracle of life and death — I noticed that I was liberated to a certain extent. In other words, my inspiration appears to be becoming less *suppressed* as I get better at *expressing* it.

Tijn: What you're saying now makes me think of the process of enlightenment.

Iebele: I hesitated for a long time about taking this liberation process as a starting point for my work, until I realized that I continued 'not to be enlightened' because I didn't have substitute metaphors at hand, in the way they were used in earlier mystical and religious expressions. The Islamic mystic Rumi wrote, for example: "I am a God of all directions." The depth of this one line is well understood by the mystics, but what is the value of this sentence in a society in which the only associations with the *concept* of the divine are raping choir boys, burning witches, and other forms of religious dictatorship? On top of that, not only have the choir boys been raped, but every spiritual stirring has been reduced to a disconcerting silence by an age-long violent and religious madness. The two World Wars may also have contributed to this. And this is how, in my opinion, we have arrived in a vacuum that makes us contemplate anew which images, metaphors, and words we can use instead of 'God.' We see concepts arise as 'all that is,' which is in fact a definition saying nothing but 'that which we don't understand, and with which we are permeated.' There are no words to describe God, as all forms of wisdom traditionally state. It is what it is. One can't make an image of God.

Tijn: I know you as an artist who is engaged mainly with consciousness and spirituality. Maybe you are inspired by God most of all, but if you have no metaphors and images how can you represent something? As you said before: you have given yourself an almost impossible task.

Iebele: Apart from the inner movement, aspiring to spiritual insight, I am also fascinated by perceptions in the material realm. In science, the latter — the empiric finding — has dominated for a long time, even to the extent that spiritual and religious considerations were banned from scientific models. In Christian terms, this has made us 'sink deeper into the dust.' To creep out of the dust, it would seem logical therefore to investigate the other direction and concentrate on the question of what happens if we rise up above the physical reality, because we humans can do that too. The miracle of life can't only be found in the body, but also, possibly thanks to the body, in what we call consciousness. We may experience more or less ecstatic moments in which all limitations of time and place blur. This is a hyper-individual experience, but it feels universal. What would happen if *everyone* lived in this ecstasy *all the time*? What would be the consequence for the perception of physical reality?

Tijn: Do you mean the experience, for example, when you seem to feel every cell of your body? That is a physical experience, but one in which you feel a connectedness of an almost cosmic order. What I find so fascinating is that you keep hammering at this experience which you are able to describe well, yet you seem to want to go even deeper, even further. Why do you want to say it even more clearly than you did already? Wasn't that enough?

Iebele: In your book, *Instant Enlightenment*, you write about a 'field' connecting all things in the universe. I understand that an image like that offers meaning to a lot of people and, to a certain extent, answers their questions about life. Suppose I wanted to use that image as an artist. Then the question of *how* is still open. That's why I want to look further; for what I'd like to know is where the movement that is happening now, this enormous focus on consciousness by millions of people, will take us. The assumption that we, as humans, create 'our own reality' with our consciousness has quite a few consequences, I think. I imagine this movement will culminate in the end in a 'culture of consciousness' like I just mentioned. I wonder to what extent such a culture will relate to whatever manifests itself materially. I like to play with the thought that in such a culture of awareness, *process* takes over from *manifestation*. By that I mean, that we humans may, in the future, interact with each other as if it were an inner process, a process that doesn't continually need to lead to practical actions, but manifests itself only when it is *really necessary*. In this thought, two images open up for me. The first is that we return to an animal-like state, in which playing, sleeping, eating, and reproduction are the only activities we value. The second image is that we only create the 'very highest.' Think of people who act and speak as if they are gods who are doing the creating. I don't know if this image is correct, but this seems to be what many people think when they talk about 'creating one's own reality.' This thought may be just a fad, which, as so often in history, will be discouraged by all kinds of miserable misfortune. Suppose, however, that we manage as humanity to develop a highly developed, ethical, creative consciousness — it would be all right with me if all of us together made a serious, maybe necessary effort. I don't have an image for the physical results of this. I only see *possibilities*, no form.

Tijn: Isn't that what is found in quantum physics; reality consists of possibilities?

Iebele: I can imagine that consciousness in fact consists of exploring an endless series of possibilities. It seems possible to me as well to dwell in the absolute immaterial domain of what I call consciousness for the sake of convenience. In older language this was called 'the heavenly.' Still the material, tangible reality can't be denied in any way. It simply is there, in front of eyes. We derive our metaphors from that tangible reality, even the metaphors we use to describe our immaterial sensations. In arts this is obvious, also in those arts that are referred to as 'abstract.' For example, Mondrian's power was that he made art works that are in themselves metaphors of a spiritual sensation. *That* is the autonomous quality of his work. Mondrian understood that esthetic experience transcends to a different domain, and he tried, even with the most far-reaching consequences, to give shape to that insight by excluding any reference to images we know from observation. Mondrian himself already said, however, that the art after him probably would take observation as a starting point again. How that was going to happen, he did not say. That is a question contemporary art is facing now, I think; a challenge that seems as old as humanity itself: namely, how can we generate transcendental experience from a work of art? As far as I'm concerned, we develop such brilliant art and science that the transcendent experience is continuous and for everyone. However mysterious our life is, we are able to develop a state of consciousness in which we seem to experience the power behind life. But we can't comprehend it in the form of knowledge. I think this saying by Hermes Trismegistus is a beautiful one: "People's poverty is their lack of knowledge. Their wealth is their knowledge of God." This tells the same story, I think, and it is thousands of years old.

Tijn: Maybe knowledge causes limitations in our experience. The moment you use words, either by reading or speaking them, you react neurologically speaking from that part of the brain that is not active during emotional sensations like compassion and love. So, even if one reads all the great texts, neurologically they don't resonate completely because the written medium, the language, hinders that. I think that is the paradox of every language. By means of words and images, one wants to open up a world that can't be experienced from the point of view of knowledge.

Iebele: I think what you have said explains why every era needs new words and images to relate the same story over and over. The word *God* for example is loaded these days with many different views and discussions. I can imagine that *God* was once the right word to name a whole range of impressions and emotions: respect, love, compassion, despair, sadness and joy, questions about life and death. For all of these, people could call on God. This God appears in literature as an omniscient insight, offering sudden understanding, or spurring us on to a loving and fiery longing for compassion. There are also stories about people who, once they stood eye to eye with God, were literally digested by his power, his overwhelming combination of terror and beauty. There are stories of people who later died of madness, but there are also stories of people who turned into great teachers after being purified by this experience. The experience of the mystical moment is a combination of sometimes very violent paradoxes that are experienced as if there is 'one source' which keeps everything moving. It's exactly like you say: words and images can't really describe this moment, however badly we may want it. In any case, the concept 'God' apparently no longer suffices in this time to name the paradoxes of a cosmic experience. In Western art and literature, we have images of biblical scenes — like Christ suffering — which have served for a long time as metaphors to express the holy moment, the moment in which life really seems to rise up from finiteness. Because religious symbols in our time are not shared generally, the inspiration behind these metaphors is expressed less often in art and literature. Mondrian solved this brilliantly, I think, by distancing himself from individual experiences in order to express the universal. In his time, that was an important starting point for him as a theosophist. He wanted to study the underlying unity of the world religions, regardless of their differences in cultural determination. Mondrian ultimately reached a purely artistic expression, without any reference to an individual experience of reality. He called this work 'neoplastic.' I would like to translate that freely into 'beyond the tangible.' In that sense, Mondrian's work is an attempt to purely spiritualize perception. Mondrian's renewal was definitely not renewal for the sake of renewal in the way we sometimes come across it in present day culture. In Mondrian's time, there was an urgent need to achieve renewal, because the spiritual, mystical sensation could no longer be depicted in old metaphors. 'The story' had to be told in a new way, in order to connect with the time.

Works in the series
Mind over Matter
2008

A strong focus on more blue quartz (detail)

From the series Mind over Matter (2008)
Psychokinesis experiment #11, 2nd sample (p = 0.275952)
Giclée print on dibond, 56 × 56 cm

I like the colored leaves in the center (Falling leaves, Bougainvillea)

From the series Mind over Matter (2008)
Psychokinesis experiment #4, 1st sample (p = 0.03196)
Giclée print on dibond, 112 × 112 cm

I prefer the light ones over the dark *(Leaves's front and back sides)*

From the series Mind over Matter (2008)
Psychokinesis experiment #5, 1st sample (p = 0.0261)
Giclée print on dibond, 112 × 112 cm

I prefer the light ones over the dark *(Hydrangea)*

From the series Mind over Matter (2008)
Psychokinesis experiment #6, 1ˢᵗ study (p = 0.0831)
Giclée print on dibond, 56 × 56 cm

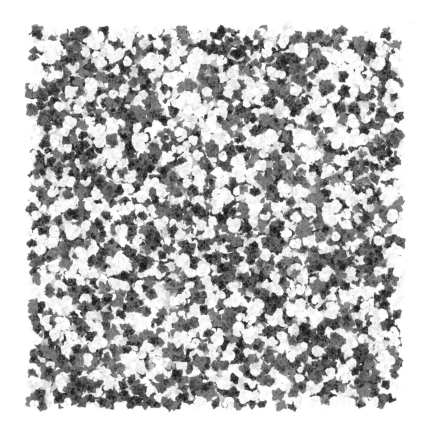

I prefer the light ones over the dark *(Hydrangea)*

From the series Mind over Matter
Psychokinesis experiment #6, 2nd study (p=0.088)
Giclée print on dibond, 56 x 56 cm

A strong focus on more blue quartz at the right side

From the series Mind over Matter (2008)
Psychokinesis experiment #11, 1ˢᵗ sample (p = 0.36677)
Giclée print on dibond, 112 × 112 cm

A strong focus on more red quartz

From the series Mind over Matter (2008)
Psychokinesis experiment #12, 4th sample (p = 0.032)
Giclée print on dibond, 112 × 112 cm

Let the living ones surround the deceased *(Red Poppies)*

From the series Mind over Matter (2008)
Psychokinesis experiment #13, 1st sample (p = 0.00087)
Giclée print on dibond, 56 × 56 cm

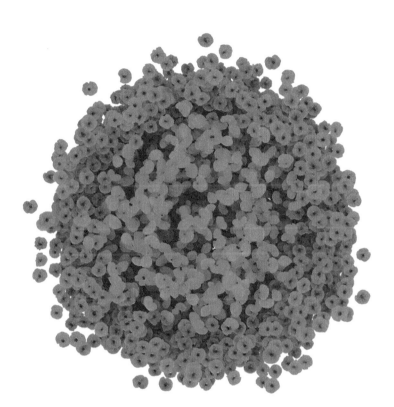

Straws bend to the right

From the series Mind over Matter (2008)
Psychokinesis experiment #17, 5th sample (p = 0.00593)
Giclée print on dibond, 56 × 56 cm

I prefer the light ones over the blue *(Hydrangea)*

From the series Mind over Matter (2008)
Psychokinesis experiment #18, 2nd sample (p = 0.004768)
Giclée print on dibond, 112 × 112 cm

The Experience of the Numinous

Conversation with Hans Gerding
Utrecht, July 2009

Hans Gerding is endowed professor of metaphysics in the spirit of theosophy at the University of Leiden and director of the Institute for Parapsychology in Utrecht. The fascination for life's mystery is an important subject in our many conversations. The conversation in this chapter deals with the numinous, the religious experience.

Hans: I think sometimes about the difference between art and advertising. There is a connection between the two because both of them use images. Some art resembles advertisements in which the holy mission of art is subordinate to making money. Much art these days is mainly about making money. The boundaries between art and advertisement have blurred, I think. What I'm beginning to miss in art is the holy mission.

Iebele: That is giving it rather a great deal of importance, a holy mission. If you make the concept 'art' too grand, you create distance. What often happens is that people make a drawing as a hobby, for example, at home. If the maker shows this to someone, he often immediately adds: "This is not art, of course." By saying that, such a person belittles the value of the drawing. It is not easy to draw the line between what is art and what isn't. Everyone has his own opinion, and as long as these opinions are respected, art offers a area of free expression. And that is exactly what most people expect of art, and I do too; let me be clear about that. But the criteria and the questions that have been developed in professional art are rather high-sounding, not only because intellectual artists often appear to have been responsible for innovation in art history. There is nothing wrong with that, and sometimes an intellectual approach is needed, but the emotional aspects that often play a role in art don't necessarily come from the intellect. By intellectually questioning the personal expression, self-evident perception and joy of art may fade. Because of differences in talent and many years of practice, one person may draw better than another. The same is true of writing poems, playing a musical instrument, and so on. Dedication, in the end, determines the skill and the value. That is the same for every trade and profession, but one doesn't say about a home-baked cake that it isn't a cake. The baker may do it better than you, but a home-made cake can be very tasty, and a cake is a cake. You don't say to a friend who has baked a good cake that you don't want it because he isn't a baker. That is how I see art. Some art reaches enormous heights, sometimes achieving the very exceptional, even 'holy' heights. And of course exceptional art may have an exceptional price. The current levels seem to be out of all proportion to the work. The art market has become a speculation market that many people look at with a healthy mistrust. I think the speculative art business will collapse one day. Tulip bulbs were a much sought-after product for speculation in the middle of the 17th century, and we all know that the prices for tulip bulbs were based on illusions at that time. The same seems to be happening with art now, although I think a work by Mondrian or Rembrandt is more valuable than a tulip bulb, of course.

Hans: The artist Jan Schoonhoven — I think he lived in Delft — had an office job, and in the evening he made his art, at home, at the dinner table. He lived like that for years. I've always thought that if I were an artist, that is how I'd do it too. A job during the day to make ends meet, keeping as much space as possible for what really matters. Then I saw a documentary about Schoonhoven's life. After he had achieved his international breakthrough, he took on a number of assistants. He made them do the things he had originally done himself, wrote 'Schoonhoven' on the back and said to the person who had made it: "Now it is worth 30,000 guilders." It has been done in this way for a long time in the artist's world, but I'm not at all happy about it.

Iebele: It may have to do with the romantic idea that an artist is someone through whom something 'supernatural' speaks; the artist then translates this something into a certain work. That particular idea is almost shamanistic, while there have also been times when art was mainly a trade. Of course, in performing a trade, outstanding craftsmanship may merge with passion and create products surpassing by far the normal levels. Yet I think, in the past the symbolism was often thought up by those commissioning the work and not by the artists themselves. In our time, that has gradually changed. Nowadays, many artists definitely use their own perceptions as starting points, almost as mediums of themselves.. That is what many people like to see: the hand of the artist. For some present-day artists, it isn't at all necessary to execute the work themselves; for them it is sufficient to clearly formulate the basic assumptions of their work. The actual trade, making the art, can be contracted out. Sol Lewitt has, for example, developed this principle since the 1970s in his Wall Drawings. He described his drawings in language, as an immaterial concept. The instructions in these texts were accurately executed by draftsmen with a highly developed feeling for both technical and artistic drawing. The hand of the artist has thus disappeared completely from the work of Sol Lewitt. By doing this, I think he spiritualized his art. And it produces images of an almost pastoral beauty.

Hans: The artist is like an architect, then. You can design churches, but you can't build them yourself. As an artist, one looks for a holy 'moment,' however. Churches are very functional in this respect: they serve as places where people can experience something holy. A lot of art is inspired by religious feelings. Now, in our time, this has changed. We say to each other from time to time: there are hardly any icons left that approach holiness.

Iebele: If you don't have any icons, you don't have any material to direct your devotion towards. When an artist paints a suffering Christ, he can put all his devotion into such a painting. The painting technique and the elements of the image serve a clear goal. A certain technique can strengthen how something is depicted. In addition to this, the artist can, if he has a personification of a godhead as his 'idiom,' draw certain figures referring to this godhead. An image becomes a narrative in this way, and makes the meaning explicit. In the current feeling about life, religious experience doesn't necessarily need the personification of a godhead, so we have lost a symbol, thus causing the expression of devotion to become more abstract. God is not an 'entity' any more. When religious experience is familiar for you, the question is relevant how you can express this experience. Without symbols, it may become a rather abstract exercise, and therefore may seem meaningless.

Hans: In your work, you reverse this question. You observed that the customary form of language no longer suffices. Yet it is not the case that people do not recognize religious feelings any more. That's why you look at the fascination people have for religious experiences in our time and you use those. You have therefore found a language form that stimulates fascination which, as Rudolf Otto puts it, evokes numinous feelings in people.

Iebele: I'm trying to do the same as Rudolf Otto did in his book *The Holy*. You recommended that book to me, and it hit the bull's eye. Otto wrote in 1917 that '*holy*' as a word obviously had no meaning any more. He observed that, in the church and in science, the significance of holiness had diminished. He tried, therefore, to bring the meaning of 'the holy' to the surface again by describing it with different concepts. He looked for different words, at a time when the common words were worn out. However, the thing that Otto wanted to express by replacing 'the holy' with 'the numinous' has not changed to this very day, in my opinion. The numinous, said Otto, is a mystery that is overwhelming, horrifying, and fascinating. I see that many people have religious feelings — I am certainly no exception — and the problem is which name one should give it. You can say: "There is more..." or you can call it spiritual, religious, or numinous, but all of this points in the end to the same experience. I think the problem is that modern science and art have moved religion to the hobby room. Religious experience doesn't seem to matter anymore in science and art. Spiritual stirring isn't taken seriously, at least not publicly. Exclusion of spiritual and religious stirrings fits perfectly in secular society. It has always amazed me that spirituality is almost absent from contemporary art.

Hans: The idea that secular society will increasingly gain ground is a misapprehension. Many random sample surveys have shown that that idea is simply untrue. It turns out that people really do want to approach life's mystery in some way or another. People look for that experience themselves. Masses of them report widely divergent experiences, which are called 'exceptional experiences' these days. The numinous aspect plays a big role here. A new language of forms is busily being sought, because many people can't experience the numinous in church anymore. Art is one way of making the numinous visible. As an art creator, you turn this around. You are looking for the spot where the numinous is hanging out these days. Obviously, the numinous is found in science, too. You settle yourself in the areas of science where the numinous lights up and you make artworks that evoke the religious experience. That is your method.

Iebele: Yes exactly. My work is often about a *method*. It is comparable to trying to become silent by meditating. The latter is the method. In the resulting silence you experience an increased depth of existence. Meditation is not a fine art, and neither is music if there is no question of material expression. Nevertheless meditation may be a method to get to know life's mystery better. What I find interesting is that some scientific disciplines obviously also reach a limit where comprehension is finite. In physics and biology, scientists arrived at the mystery, too: big questions and seemingly unsolvable paradoxes. I have tried to bring the paradoxes of quantum physics into my studio. I wanted to repeat experiments and experience those paradoxes. Doing that has not yet led to any works of art. There is still no manifestation. I haven't yet created anything which is visible or communicable. To reach that stage, I need to record something and make the connection with the mysterious aspect I want to show.

Hans: Such paradoxes also allow you to experience silence. I think a fundamental issue in your work, which stimulates the numinous, is the moment of silence. It is withdrawing yourself into the now. In your work, there is a strong 'now moment' and in that now moment a number of things come together. An old divination technique like the I Ching, for example, works with throwing coins while thinking about a question at the same time. The question and throwing the coins both carry the quality of that now-moment. In that moment, the connection is laid between the question and the coincidental process that lets the coins drop in a certain heads-tails combination. The outcome of that coincidental process is the code in the I Ching that points out the answer to your question. The intention of the question and the dropping of the coins are inextricably connected with the quality of that now moment. The connection is mysterious and that is where the numinous is hidden. It's interesting to note that modern parapsychology has found indications of an experimental subject's intentions being reflected in the behavior of a random number generator. Parapsychology has made the functioning of divination techniques empirically plausible. Referring to this, Jung said it exactly points to what he calls *unus mundus*. There is one world in which two sides of the coin behave like a unity. Amazingly, parapsychology seems to confirm this in an empirical manner, but it remains mysterious nevertheless; a fascinating mystery that indeed embraces some of what Rudolf Otto calls 'the holy,' 'the numinous.' In your work you freeze the now moment in which this mystery manifests itself. You save this moment in a technological and in an aesthetic way.

Iebele: The point of departure is not only aesthetic or technological. Deep down it is also about ethics, about life and death. Quantum processes are totally beyond control, so in working with them, even if my attention is focused very strongly on a certain result, the exact outcome is unpredictable. I can't control how my work will turn out. It is just like daily life, actually. I look for harmony and connectedness in my life but I also know that uncontrollable horrors are unavoidable. I'm longing for a good, joyful life, without pain; that is what I strive for. I try to avoid what is really painful or horrible. I think many people do that. But if you stand eye-to-eye with reality — the way it presents itself in a mystical experience — you may get something of a shock. The numinous can also be scary because of the enormous depth, the infinity. Everything is there, all extremes. Rudolf Otto writes about this and that makes him credible as far as I'm concerned. I think the criticism many people have of religion is that, to them, it is a flight from reality. It makes the world more beautiful than it seems, serving only as a consolation in a world full of uncertainty. For me, religious experience reaches further than that. The numinous is a sudden insight into terror and beauty at the same time. It is my personal choice as a human being not to want to contribute to terror, but terror cannot be denied. Death is everywhere, but so is life. That is the mysterious paradox, with maybe as a final lesson that death and life are one and the same. The numinous recognizes life and death.

Hans: Yes, the falling away of apparent limits carries a numinous moment. Parapsychology talks about interconnectedness, some kind of subterranean bonding. People experience themselves as being separate from each other, and as finite, but they are connected with each other and also with the rest of the world to a greater degree than they think and know. The holy moment in which this interconnectedness is determined arouses something as it were, that was always there, but from which we are disconnected in our consciousness. The individual consciousness is only part of the psychological reality. At the level of consciousness, many people experience separation, while interconnectedness is positively present all the time, but often invisibly. When, as you just said, during a now moment in which you produce an artwork using a random event generator, this result assumes a form which is in line with your intention. In such cases, the quantifiable aspect is interesting and draws our attention. The random event generator shows, namely, that the deviation from pure chance is indeed significant. There appears to be interconnectedness, and that is extraordinary.

Iebele: That interconnectedness is apparently a familiar feeling, and above that, it is an experience of beauty: the aesthetic of an experience that feels real. What I think is so special about this, is that such experience of beauty is completely internal. It is *inside* me. It has no form. That is what I mean when I say that there are no icons or symbols to depict this experience. Discovering interconnectedness is an inner process. Artistically speaking, one can wonder how an intangible process can still be transferred into form. Giving form to an inner process without employing icons and form criteria feels like being artistically inconvenienced, but it is also liberating to enter an area that is still completely open to artistic exploration.

We have rules in order to survive together in society. If you project the interconnectedness experience on to our society, all kinds of constructions that have been thought up to enable us to survive seem to matter a lot less. In the long-established tradition of art, all kinds of principles have been thought up for how image and music should come into being. All traditions shape themselves by piling rules upon rules upon rules. In the experience of interconnectedness — call it a mystical experience of god or enlightenment — all those constructions appear to be unnecessary for reaching that experience! I start out from the assumption that the quality of such an experience of interconnectedness may 'jump' over to the artwork when this is produced in the now moment of inspiration. The artwork may generate this experience again in someone who later looks at or listens to it. If this happens, that is the artistic value of the work.

Hans: A number of your artworks from the series *Mind over Matter* clearly exceeded the probability. The statistical chance of the images in this series getting the patterns you wanted is very small. This low probability is clearly visible to everyone in the 'language' of this series. Interconnectedness has been proven because the frozen now moment in which it arose shows a relationship between your intention and the significant deviation in the behavior of the quantum parts in your random event generator that produced the image.

Iebele: That's why the combination with the title is important for the images from the series *Mind over Matter*. The title and the work form an autonomous didactic treatise, enabling the public to analyze the work: one can see that the title indicates exactly what the image is. Working with a title to give meaning to the work is often used in the fine arts. I mentioned Sol Lewitt earlier. In his work, the title had a similar descriptive meaning. In my series *Mind over Matter*, the title 'Straws bend to the right,' for example, indicates that it was my intention in this work to have all straws bend to the right. The image shows that it worked. The observer may deduce that this work is also a successful psychokinetic experiment. The combination of title and work enables people to infer, for a moment, that it has been possible to evoke the mystical situation in which 'spirit was breathed into dust.' That's why this series has been called *Mind over Matter*, of course.

Hans: The numinous moment is presented in this series in a very unambiguous way.

Iebele: The language of images I used to present this moment could have been very different, however. People often ask me: "Why did you choose this form exactly?" One way I deal with the language of images is to take my first inspiration seriously by cherishing it as something of great value. When this project first took shape in my mind, I wanted to do something with boulders and leaves. I'm always dumbfounded by the quantity of leaves and boulders in the world. In whatever pattern I find them, they always seem to have a natural order in nature, as if coincidence has played no role. I wanted to try to get to a similar order in a technical environment, touched, injected, by consciousness. The only way to realize this was to set up the technique very purely, very precisely. If I want my consciousness to have an influence on the way boulders and leaves are projected onto a sheet of paper in a virtual machination, the technique has to be perfect first. With a messy technique you can't judge if a correlation exists between my consciousness and the machines generating the images. And that is what I was after. The ultimate image had to radiate the same infallible accuracy as the technique being used. I have worked for over a year to get the technique straight. In applying this pleasant form of perfectionism, I chose not to get it wrong. I wanted to do it as well as I could.

Hans: Out of respect for the process.

Iebele: Yes, exactly. I wanted to be sure that the machine generating the quantum noise worked, and that this noise was evaluated reliably into an image. Software has been developed especially for this project, which wasn't simple. Dick Bierman helped me very patiently with this, because I had never done such a thing. In fact, I was doing a scientific experiment for the first time in my life. I wanted to photograph the pebbles and leaves I used in the images as sharply as possible. The result, the resulting image of an experiment, I wanted to print with the greatest possible color depth, on paper which keeps as long as possible. I chose crystal glass, which allows every detail to be clearly visible. The black frame has a purpose too. The work in the series *Mind over Matter* was a 'framed' process, literally, in time and technique. The process that mattered to me occurred inside that frame within a few minutes and in technical surroundings of wires and computers. In the end, quite apart from all these considerations, I could have chosen a very different form. I think the first inspiration, and the measure of care and patience with which this inspiration has been elaborated, is an important criterion for the quality of an artwork. That aspect alone has a value, quite apart from the meaning.

Hans: I think the care you took to set up the surroundings in which your artworks could arise is an expression of respect for the process.

Iebele: Yes, and respect for the moment in which the works arose. The moments in which inspiration and manifestation go hand in hand are really rare. These have been marvelous moments, which I will never forget.

Hans: That is an important point. In the series *Mind over Matter* you literally show that interconnectedness has been at work. And even though it was not your first intent, you were able to support this with scientific arguments. But I have the idea that you have taken a different path since you made the series *Mind over Matter*. First you wanted to convince yourself of interconnectedness by producing artworks. You have done that in a creative process that deviates significantly from chance in an expressive way. Now you seem to have

One Seagull (2009)

Psychokinesis experiment #20
Giclée print on dibond, 108 × 108 cm

arrived at some sort of acceptance of interconnectedness. Given this acceptance, the surpassing of chance expectation plays a lesser role now.

Iebele: What you say is exactly what formed the starting point for 'One Seagull,' the image with the enormous flock of seagulls. I had the computer randomly select several photos of one single flying seagull and place each photo randomly into a spatial computer model. Such a positioning based on chance may turn out many different ways, of course. I expected — and that is important in this context — that by following this process attentively, the final image would arise, more or less representing my 'idea' of a swarm of seagulls. I did this test just once, and it hit the mark right away. A splendid flock of seagulls appeared in a frame that was set up beforehand. The work became a perfect expression of how I like to look at those birds when I stand on the beach. I have reduced the process of making an artwork to observing the arising of an image, in order to arrive at an image which corresponds with the observation of the reality itself. I took interconnectedness for granted. It is like painting without a brush. By not touching the material anymore, I can begin as purely as possible with the consciousness in order to create a universal experience. But the point of departure is observation; otherwise 'nothing' would be there.

Hans: That is almost platonic. You want to make a deeper reality visible. Plato's thought is that a birch tree you see is what it is, thanks to the idea 'birch treeness' which is the foundation of all birch trees in the world. Schopenhauer said that the artist who paints a birch tree makes an artwork if he paints that birch tree in such a way that the idea of 'birch treeness' shimmers through it. That world of ideas in Schopenhauer's philosophy isn't visible for everyone in the everyday world; it is a deeper reality. The interesting aspect of your work is that it engages art and science at the same time. The whole point is exploring ways that lead to knowledge. According to Schopenhauer — and that's why he is so popular among artists — an artwork is cognitive. It is knowledge of reality, particularly of a deeper reality of which science only describes the surface. That's how it is with your projects. Something eternal, hiding behind the phenomenon, filters through.

Iebele: Wanting to look; wanting to look at all costs at the deeper reality, which is, as far as I'm concerned, the basis of our life, is the field of art where I feel most at home.

Hans: Your work wants to stimulate the spectator to discover meaning. Your work, therefore, is always communicative. Every artist wants to communicate of course, but your work generates 'meaning' in the form of interconnectedness and numinousness. I mean, 'the numinous,' as defined by Rudolf Otto, something mysterious, overwhelming, horrifying and fascinating. By 'fascinating,' Otto means gripping, in the double sense of the word that it doesn't only attract one's attention, but also holds it.

Iebele: I easily recognize that 'fascinating' in the meaning Otto gave to it: your attention is attracted and held. The numinous doesn't let you go. You want to go there again and again, and it holds you in a grip as if you are sucked into it, even if you don't know where it will take you. Sometimes it is an almost scary surrender to life. I find it hard to express this in images, maybe because the icons we talked about earlier are missing. The numinous is like a decomposing corpse with flowers growing on it, while you know you yourself are that corpse. All of us will end that way. When you surrender, your own death doesn't harm you anymore, for life's continuation without one's body is a certainty. My body will provide the building material for another being, in the same way that I was made from material that once formed other beings. Even my own body goes through this. My cells die continuously and new ones keep growing. I also experience interconnectedness in that principle.

Hans: You found a special form of expression for this cycle and the boundary between life and death.

Iebele: At a certain moment, I experienced the need to express that boundary. That is why I have designed an 'oracle' which uses generated coincidence. The aim in this case is that the public interacts with this automatic oracle. For this oracle, I have used old biblical texts containing the principles which Otto mentioned. The text I used as a basis for the oracle, *Ecclesiastes*, was written by Qohelet, the author of the book Preacher. Like all good literature, this text is full of rock-hard conflicts and paradoxes. I have tried to put them into a contemporary framework. Qohelet didn't get to the bottom of life's secrets and he indicated specifically why not. Addressing oneself to the paradoxes and seeming aimlessness of life produces an insight that can't be fully described by any word or image. Not 2000 years ago, not now.

Hans: Your oracle project fits very well in the divination techniques of ancient wisdom traditions. It is a literal example of prognostication, because you take coincidence and interconnectedness as a point of departure. You stand opposite the oracle. The oracle starts to speak. The coincidence by which the oracle starts to speak in your installation can definitely be put between quotation marks. The oracle in fact says something to you. That happens in the frozen 'now moment' we talked about earlier. The quality of your presence in the now moment is reflected in the coincidence process of that same now moment. In your installation it leads to the oracle speaking a text that is addressed literally to you personally.

Iebele: You're right. I don't raise the matter of the presence of interconnectedness or a cosmic order with this oracle any more, although I was still doing so in the series *Mind over Matter*. I now just use it. It is extraordinary hearing a woman speak without having to ask a question. I'm simply assuming that the woman's text has a meaning at the moment she says a verse and that this is based on coincidence. The beautiful thing in Qohelet's story is that everything he wrote is based on previous personal experience. It is not an *a priori* intellectual position. It is a *video a posterior* experience: 'I observe after the experience.' Real emotional life comes after experience. That, the feeling, is real. We may claim this feeling as a reality because it follows the experience. Nowadays this is something that especially women demand.

Hans: Yes, that is why it is nice that the oracle is a woman. It used to be like that, and now it is like that again.

Iebele: There has been a discussion about Qohelet being a man or a woman. After years of debate and research we now assume he was a man after all. But Qohelet spoke in his time remarkably respectfully about women. He said for example: "I heard many stories about women being thoroughly bad." He had never experienced anything which proved that women were even a hair less than men, however.

Ecclesiastes (2009)

An automated oracle based on the texts of Qohelet, using electronic divination techniques
Still from video projection
Written, designed and directed by Iebele Abel
Performed by Lyndsey Housden

At the end of the Old Testament someone speaks in the person of Qohelet, who cannot and does not want to explain away disdain for women. I think Qohelet had not yet found the more explicit words with which Christ expressed himself later. I think Christ introduced love for fellow beings as something that really exists, and that is why it could become an essential guideline. Love for the other, is a typical female 'attribute' too. I think after Christ, God gradually became a safer spot in the universe. With Christ's God, there was space for female safety and forgiveness in addition to male wrath and authority. In our time, we witness how this aspect of the divine is expressed by the thought that we may feel ourselves to be carried by the universe, that we are cells of one large cosmic body. A starting point like that makes the necessity of love for fellow human beings very clear and understandable. I think Qohelet was looking for similar words, but he couldn't reconcile all of this with the unavoidable death, which seems to make all our searching and drudgery meaningless. In our time we are searching too. We are searching for concepts that interpret both our experience of unity and separateness. I like to have an oracle say all kinds of everyday paradoxes via a technique that knows these paradoxes too; the paradox of quantum mechanics, which implies one cannot say anything about something until it has been observed. Your contact with the oracle does not exist until you have seen and heard the woman speak that one 'coinciding' text. Moreover, I also want to show a paradox of history with my installation 'Ecclesiastes': nothing appears to be really new while new things keep coming.

Hans: There is meaning in searching for and working with interconnectedness. There is a strong fascination for this, in a variety of study fields. Jung said, for example, that subjects in parapsychological experiments who aim to make interconnectedness visible, are in a heightened state of emotionality. According to Jung, this is because the researcher who guides the subject seriously assumes that that subject is able to make a miracle happen. If a researcher seriously expects that interconnectedness can be demonstrated, it appears sooner in the subject. Jung said about that: "Every person has his thoughts about miracles. Every person has the hope to finally witness a miracle."

Iebele: Zen master Genpo Merzel asked his children questions as an experiment, at a certain moment, as if they were very wise. His children gave amazingly wise answers, obviously because they were addressed as wise people. Inspired by this experience, Genpo Merzel has developed a psychological method which he calls *Big Mind*. As soon as you give people space to develop themselves completely, it often happens. This tells us quite a lot about all the education and social systems that assume people, and especially children, wouldn't know what is good for them.

Hans: Yes, whereas we do 'somehow' know what is good for us. We are already home but we have forgotten it. There are obstacles blocking the way to a wider view and thus to a deeper understanding. Removing these obstacles and blocks has always been a beautiful assignment.

Iebele: I think more in terms of replacing obstacles than in removing them, as you said. These obstacles are some kind of stop sign, red traffic lights. One could replace them with direction indicators. It must be possible to find alternatives for these obstacles, by viewing the moments of blocking as moments of choice and possibility. In that way you keep the road open to further development. By building big obstacles, like in the school system in which children are locked away from what fascinates them because they can't read or do math well, one creates suppression. Of course, we have been educated like that too. At school and in our careers, we have to perform within the norms of society even though we didn't establish them ourselves. Because of that, we aren't used to establishing our own norms in our own development, either. However, I see more and more people who, especially as they get older, want to follow their own feelings and fascinations. The social order can only partially provide support for personal inner development right now. For those who easily participate in a society that aims for the most part at welfare, comfort and status, this may not cause a problem. In my mind it is really a matter of 'social Darwinism.' Only the people who are able to fulfill the high demands of a social career — and who don't fundamentally put the social system up for discussion either — find financial comfort and personal satisfaction in such a career. Those who don't fulfill the demands of society, get isolated fairly soon. One could say it is their own fault. Possibly, but it could also be the system's fault. I tend to think the latter. After all, present-day society demands that all the cogs in the system work properly. This model is based on a technological metaphor, as if people are machines within a larger machine.

Hans: It looks like the balance has been lost for that reason.

Iebele: I think many people are longing for a new form of society; one that takes fellow humans, animals and the Earth into account. That's why I expect people to step out of the present system and start investigating new forms of society. The anarchist Noam Chomsky, in referring to this topic, said that if one decides to plant one's own garden instead of eating from the garden of the oppressed, one in fact decides to live as a moral being instead of as a monster[1]. Moral beings, according to Chomsky, are those who feel responsible for what they do and what they don't do. We know the motives of a monster by now: greed, hate, and violence. But what are the motives of a moral being? What is it inside us that wants to do well? This question brings me back to the mystery. I can understand evil as a reaction to an awkward situation, but I don't know the origin of love. It feels like love is of a higher order than 'evil.' Isn't that how it *feels*?

Hans: Entering those unfamiliar domains like you do in your work — thus making them visible — is recognizable for many people. The unknown is fascinating because it also gives freedom. It stimulates a longing for knowledge which you expect to be there but which has not been experienced yet. If you come close to this knowledge, however, you do recognize it. Therefore, approaching life's mystery is a numinous experience. It is a memory of knowledge you already possess. That is platonic too: knowledge is memory.

Iebele: It is a very special circle. You can experience such a memory during a conversation. We are experiencing this memory right now, just by talking about it. And yet we are in that circular movement all the time, because we also come *out* of the memory, that feeling of deep connectedness and deep knowledge. I wonder sometimes if that movement will ever stop. On the one hand, I can imagine your striving for total enlightenment for everyone and achieved by everyone. The only human thing you can do is to aspire to that, at least in my mind. On the other hand, I can hardly imagine that such

---

1 See chapter 8 of *Chomsky on Anarchism*, Barry Pateman (ed.), AK Press Edinburg, 2005.

80

a state of being — enlightenment — will ever be reached collectively, because why hasn't it already happened in all those thousands of years of human history? I could also imagine it may well have been reached at some point in the past, because where else would the longing for liberation come from? Maybe this freedom is hidden in our memories, like you said. Every era demands anew a contemporary expression, a specific articulation of our need for the freedom experience.

Hans: Yes, that is the assignment: working towards more freedom. I'm convinced of that, and you'll find out if you just let it happen. What can be discovered philosophically, one can read in many books. Plato's grotto myth is a good example. Humans are chained, limited, ignorant, and sleepy. Liberation is possible, but reading about it in a book is not what it is all about. Instead, it is about executing what has been described to us.

Iebele: That isn't a simple assignment, though. One never achieves full understanding and full liberation.

Hans: Jung said it is about encircling the center. You can approach life's mystery, and if you approach it, you recognize it as such. In every new era, people have to discover that in their own way. Not merely by reading about it. 'Approaching' it is an assignment to become who you are.

Iebele: I get the distinct impression that children aren't stimulated to search for the mystery. At school, they learn more especially the 'certainties': languages, grammar, math, Western cosmology. Of course this is basic material for one's general development, but children often go through a phase in which they simply don't believe that the cosmology they learn in school is right. Has there ever been a big bang? What was there, then, before the big bang? Or in Christian cosmology: what was there before God? These questions are unsolvable, but I think many children would benefit from acknowledging this mystery; searching for the mystery doesn't stop with 'we don't know.' I Precisely that — the realization that we don't know 'it' — seems to me to be fundamental in achieving a better understanding. It gives an open, investigative attitude. If we recognize that the mystery is ultimately much greater than our knowing, a flower becomes just as valuable as the 'I.' If you do not know who God is, you will not take it into your head to want to convert someone; neither will you, as happens now, want to install a uniform global banking system or 'democracy.' This is because you can't know that that system is better than another one. The same is true for materialistic thinking, which is so dominant. Every imaginary experience of a child is dismissed as fantasy, as if it didn't exist. Only that which we can 'cut into slices,' is told in our educational system to be true. If we do not recognize feelings or fantasy, we are suppressing freedom. Why do you think it is suppressed like that? Why do so many people have the feeling they have to keep their mouths shut about an experience that has touched them deeply? People who have experienced God, for example, or who have talked with God. Such mystic experiences are often clothed with a certain shame, while such an experience may well have a deep significance.

Hans: There are many sides to this. The path leading to an approach to life's mystery is a process. That process may be dangerous. On that path or in that process, many accidents happen because there are all kinds of pitfalls. Above the gate, giving access to that road, is written in big letters: 'Know thyself.' The process guiding us to self knowledge is tough. First, you are confronted with the shadow — in other words, your negative side. It is very difficult to face that. Then some things are revealed to you, but while you are on your path, you change so much that you might fall into a trap or down a precipice. You may become mad. You may exercise power over other people or over nature and you may handle that the wrong way, too. These are all pitfalls. There is an urge to explore the unknown but, at the same time, society tends to urge people to be cautious. The self knowledge, conservative powers say, will come later. That happens if we die and go to heaven, and if we have lived decently and followed the rules. Those conservative powers are there with a purpose, because people want to protect themselves against the numinous, for it is overwhelming, and terrifying. On the other hand, however, there is the question: how do you stay alive within the stifling regulations that want to encase the numinous?

Iebele: Yes indeed, if you guard the numinous too rigorously, life loses its shine, and maybe even its meaning. When I started to express my fascination for life's mystery explicitly in my work, I knew I was crossing a certain boundary. I was liberating myself from the grip of the conservative powers that, for years, had kept me from expressing my deepest fascinations. That was liberating of course. However,

I felt an enormous uncertainty because I had no answer to all the questions the mystery evokes. The mystery only gets bigger. Why would I want to express it? I did it anyway, for the stifling regulations you mentioned became too limiting for me. However well I looked, my question about the mystery, my looking for God, simply could not find a satisfactory breeding ground in the secular, technological society of today. I wanted the deeper meaning of life to be discussible, even though I don't know what that meaning is. Even if that meaning isn't there at all, life's miracle still moves me so strongly that I can't but recognize that this miracle is my deepest motive. Luckily, I found a connection among physics, parapsychology, mysticism and my artistic work for my study of the miracle. When I first presented the series *Mind over Matter*, I thought I would receive a lot of criticism for the work. I thought maybe people would find my use of scientific methods to bring the spiritual into art ridiculous or not 'artistic' enough, but exactly the opposite happened. Many people recognize precisely my fascination for the ungraspable and the mysterious. They find it liberating that spirituality can have a present-day figurative or musical expression. That was a considerable relief to me — that so many people are looking for the same thing I am. Some people may search for their uniqueness, but I don't want to be special at all. I ask for nothing better than finding the similarities between myself and other people.

Hans: I think that is precisely the strength of your work. You express the numinous moment in such a way that it is accessible. There is a need for that because numinous feelings are alive and kicking.

Iebele: That numinous moment calls forth enthusiasm, but it may also be pictured too beautifully, too harmoniously. The experience of interconnectedness has a certain beauty, but it can also be terrifyingly vast. Let me put it this way: in all traditions, people who have experienced the numinous come out of it more or less scared at first. After that, a process begins in which one makes choices. One chooses a path. Do you want to be someone who brings about genocide or do you want to be someone who takes care of the victims that result? Both courses of life are in God. That is the scary part of the numinous. God is everything, including the most terrible and terrifying experiences.

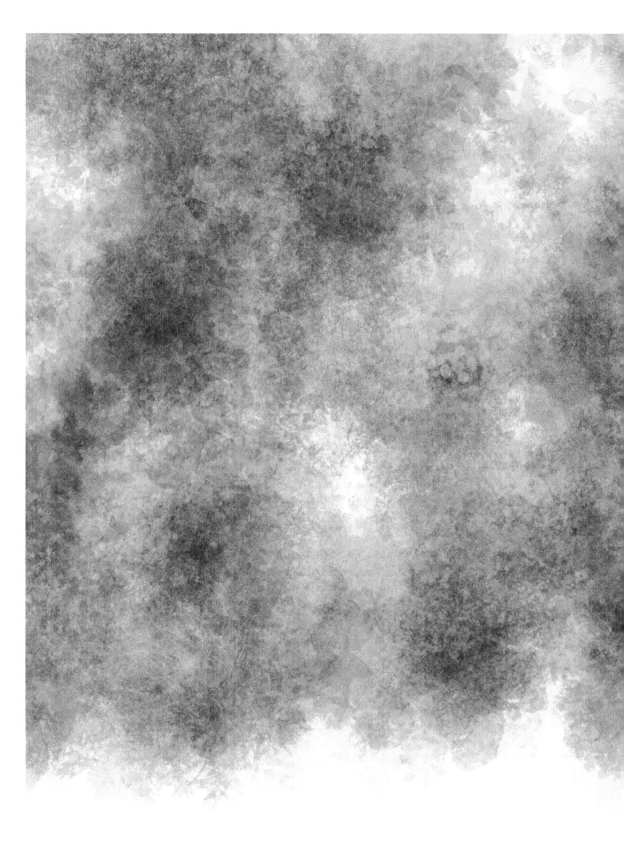

Mind Garden — Mediatation on Death (2009)

Psychokinesis experiment #21 (detail panel 1)
Giclée print on dibond, 7 panels, 187 × 54 cm

Mind Garden — Meditation on Death (2009)
Psychokinesis experiment #21
Giclée print on dibond, 7 panels, 187 × 54 cm

Photo: Pulchri Studio, The Hague (2009)

Hans: I think most of us have a rather vague notion of spirituality. Spirituality is often avowed in a pious way: cozy and beautiful, as in a fairy tale. Spirituality is, in essence, a purification process that has painful and difficult sides to it, and makes you more awake. I think art is a matter of expressing spirituality in such a way that everyone gets out of it what for him or her has a real power of expression at that moment. As Jung said about the Holy Mass in the Catholic Church: those who really understand, know that it is about living, dying, rising again, and being reborn during their lifetime. You have to do something about it yourself instead of waiting until you die. That is scary for many people, however, and that is why it is kept at a distance with the story that Jesus does all of that for you. You don't die during your life then, but at the end of your physical life, after which heaven is waiting.

Iebele: Some people see that churches and even religion in general mislead them with such a simplified story. The story of heaven after death is the carrot offered to us so we will lead a decent life. And that is definitely how it has been. But the path you just described has a certain sympathy. With relatively simple, and not too scary symbols, an opening is offered to make a move towards the mystery and to learn more about it.

Hans: Absolutely. Those who get a little further, and follow the Path as far as they can, find support in these traditions themselves. Jung's psychology says that a final process is unfolding in human beings. A process striving to reach a goal, aiming at something. That goal is waking up. One gets to real maturity at some point, which includes starting to cooperate consciously with that waking up process. The question is then: how seriously do you want to take that process and how far do you want to go?

Iebele: That complete wakefulness can make me cheerful, but it can also arouse an almost dispirited neutrality. By neutrality, I mean that one attributes the same value to everything. Nothing has more value than anything else. I notice that I myself choose a certain point of view. If I could preview what my choices would lead to, I'd rather do things that support life than things that undermine life. In my experience, that is what works best in the end. I don't want to live with knowingly having caused pain. I don't like that, but that has nothing to do with wisdom. In my work, I have always chosen a safe numinousness, as it were. I know the horrors, but I don't explicitly show them, because I don't strive for horrors.

Hans: I'm a great believer in common sense in this respect. You can read all kinds of things and go in search of information, but you still have your own personal way. You have to make choices if you arrive at an intersection: one path goes *here*, the other one *there*. Often you can more or less recognize where a certain path will lead to. You take the path that feels good, but where it leads to exactly, you don't know. You gauge your intentions but you can't see where they'll lead you. You try to get your intentions as pure as possible and thus your deeds, too. You are not responsible for where your deeds lead you. You offer all your deeds devotedly and trustingly.

Iebele: Once, I was waiting on an empty platform late at night, and I had big and complicated problems to solve. While I was walking along that platform, I stopped at a certain moment and thought: gee, the solution for my problems is that, from now on, I can try to do it right. I didn't know at that moment what 'right' would be, but the decision to choose the right solution, whatever the cost, was a real choice. It certainly had to do with devotion. I didn't know what I was going to do, but I decided to weigh up my choices — the good against the wrong ones. That was close to a religious experience; I thought I saw 'the path to the light' for one moment.

Hans: Yes, that is interesting. You set your choice alongside 'something.' You test something in such a choice. You make an appeal to something. It is a communicative moment.

Iebele: I still don't know, however, what I compare my choices with.

Hans: I don't either. You don't know what it is you compare your choices with, and yet it is with 'something.'

Iebele: That 'something' touches me deeply.

Hans: I find that emotion a characteristic of your work. In good faith, you hand over all control to that 'something' at the most sacred moment in the creative process — the numinous 'now moment' — the flash in which an artwork suddenly appears from nowhere, after all your long and patient preparations.

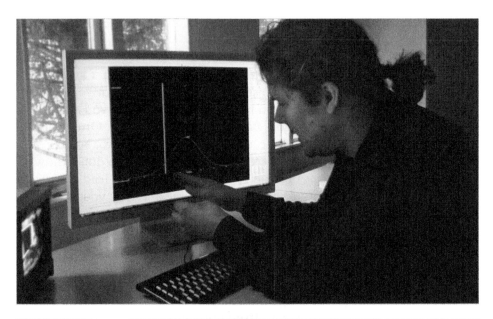

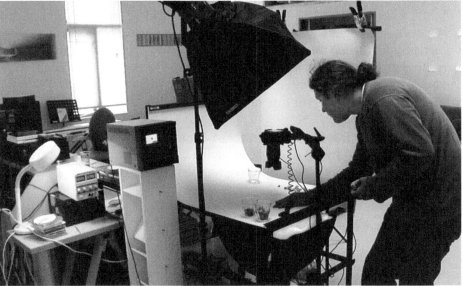

The first photograph depicts an experiment in which I try to move the vertical line to the left by means of mind focus (see also page 12). The second photograph is taken in my studio while capturing stones, leaves and straws for the works in the series Mind over Matter (2008).

A Natural Law of Consciousness

Conversation with Roger Nelson, Princeton, June 2009

Dr. Roger Nelson is an experimental psychologist and founding director of the Global Consciousness Project. The GCP was established in 1998 as an international, multidisciplinary collaboration of scientists, engineers, and artists. The project consists of collecting data from a global network of random generators located in 65 cities around the world, for the purpose of looking for subtle correlations that may reflect the presence of a globally active consciousness. When millions of people have common thoughts and emotions, the 65 random generators worldwide indicate small but meaningful differences from the normal structure. During the attacks on the World Trade Center on September 11 in New York, a remarkable deviation was registered too, making a reasonable case for the consciousness of a large number of people having a measurable impact on physical reality. GCP is the first research project of its kind to be set up on such a large scale, and it led to other similar projects, particularly after the publications about 9/11. Roger Nelson's research and publications have contributed considerably to knowledge and understanding of seemingly hidden qualities of our consciousness.

Iebele: When we first met, we got into quite a spontaneous exchange right away. After all, both of us work with the same machinery and methods, and you have a marked interest in the way data from random generators may be used to make music and images. It is clear to us that if art is made this way, there is a non-material interface with consciousness. Not everyone will find it as self evident as we do, for we use rather specific means and we can't expect everyone to be familiar with those. I have noticed that working with REGs appears to make it possible to catch moments of heightened inspiration in an image or sound. The results of this way of working often arouse a perception of interconnectedness in the public. In my work, I look for ways to bring forth the connectedness with a cosmic order. I have noticed that — quite apart from the artworks themselves — talking about this subject causes a certain shift of consciousness. Mentioning the interconnectedness often suffices to bring forth the experience. Talking about the theory behind it and the technique I use is not always necessary, but sometimes it is. Without the underlying theory and technology, my work would not exist after all. The exchanges with others on the subject bring forth deepening. That is why I like to talk about it, but how can you do this in an accessible way?

Roger: When I write about my work there are two modes. I may tell what I think, or I may tell what I imagine a reader would like to know. The difference may sound slight, but it is important because the connection with others actually creates something new. It is a collaboration, and even when the extra source is actually within my own mind, it activates different patterns of thought and reveals aspects that might otherwise remain hidden. A live conversation, even a presentation to an audience, uses energy from both parties, and because there is interaction, I think there is potentially a shared consciousness that models this subtle thing we both are studying. The creativity in a collaboration is different, sometimes more powerful or effective, sometimes not, but always ready to tap into synergies that suggest the old saying, "two heads are better than one."

Iebele: You mean that you not only achieve more, on a physical level, when working together, but that working together, talking, brainstorming, also has an effect on another level. It changes our consciousness. We change by exchanging information, however ungraspable information may be.

Roger: I think your art is aimed in the same direction — exploring the active creative capacity of mind and intention. This is an important matter for the world at large because we do have capabilities we are not generally using because we don't yet realize their power. When we focus and direct our minds to affect the world, it changes. Your artworks exhibit this directly by creating patterns that would not exist except for your intent. The world needs this now because there is so much difficult work to do that can be accomplished only if we cooperate and collaborate and assume responsibility to match our creativity.

Iebele: I think there is a growing understanding of mutual connectedness these days. In spite of this, the connection between consciousness and the physical reality we live in is mysterious. I wanted to investigate the relationship between perception and consciousness years ago with an EEG, which is used for clinical purposes as well. In those days, I saw such a machine as a sensor of consciousness. When I transferred an EEG signal into music that was especially made for this purpose, my consciousness reacted to it and the reverse also happenend: the music reacted to my changed state of consciousness. In this set up, I was wired up to the machines. It was the presence of the wires, in particular, that made it more or less understandable for the public. Later on, when I started to work with REGs, it became much harder to explain what I was doing. One of the reasons is that I don't understand exactly how consciousness and REGs seem to react to each other. As far as I know, *nobody* understands that. In spite of this, a music installation based on an REG seems to affect my consciousness in a similar way as when I use an EEG. It is still a mystery, however, why an REG seems to be sensitive to changes of consciousness without being connected to the body in any way.

Roger: Consciousness and mind are not simply an extrusion of brain activity, and are not confined to your head. Mind extends out into the world and may interact and have direct effects in the world. I think almost all people will recognize a special new presence in the world when we meet someone and fall in love. The two people, originally individuals, change a little, and give over a part of the individuality to create something new, the couple. There is a consciousness field that develops between and around that couple, which is made from their two interacting consciousness fields. If they are strangers, their fields merely interpenetrate, but when common experiences, shared thoughts, and emotions develop, there is a growth of interaction; there is coincident, correlated, and synchronized mental activity. This produces a new, shared field of consciousness. Ripples and waves in their personal fields enter into a dance. They are now a new entity, a bonded pair.

Iebele: And obviously this consciousness dance does not only appear between people, but also between people and machines. Then consciousness becomes very concrete, very tangible then. The machine, in our case the super-fast electronic head-or-tails machine, indicates in ranges of numbers when a consciousness dance happens. At least that is what appears to be the case.

Roger: In laboratory experiments with random event generators (REGs), which can be thought of as high-speed electronic coin flippers, we ask people to try to get more heads, or more tails. They succeed, slightly, and over many repetitions in rigorously controlled experiments, we demonstrate that the output of the REG isn't random when people try to change it, but shows a tiny, but statistically significant effect of the mental effort to change its behavior. Now, back to the loving couple for a moment. We ask what happens when two people who are bonded in this way try together to affect the REG. Their effect is much stronger than either individual can produce. Why might that be? We can't say for certain, but I think it is plausible that because they are a couple, they have the experience of mental and emotional interaction we identify as bonding or love, and they can apply this immediately relevant experience in the attempt to interact with the REG.

Iebele: You mentioned consciousness *field*. The concept 'field' is often used nowadays as a metaphor for the interaction between humans, animals, and things; not only on a physical level, but more and more in the context of our consciousness. The 'field' has become a concept in the spiritual perception of many people. Research like yours has brought forth scientific material showing that interconnectedness may be the case, both materially and spiritually. I understand that the concept 'field' is an obvious term to unify diverse spiritual schools with the exact sciences, but at the same time I think the concept is confusing too. Energy and power fields have a totally different meaning in physics than the interconnectedness experience of consciousness, but they are vaguely attributed to an exchange of energy. These kinds of fields seem to be more or less the same, while in fact it is not known at all which variables play a role in consciousness. I like to think about the possibility of developing a 'natural law of consciousness,' in spiritually intuitive as well as in scientific terms. In this way, a more encompassing and, in particular, a more correct description of the way in which consciousness is experienced and how it relates to our physical existence would become available. I think there is a need to express consciousness as an autonomous 'entity,' for the simple reason that we seem to experience our consciousness as such. I imagine that in such a 'natural law of consciousness,' the capital C (for consciousness, of course) is the variable. For the time being the comparison is still C = ? Consciousness is a question mark.

Roger: I applaud your suggestion, not least because I would like to do something similar. We know from research in laboratories over decades, and from work like that of the GCP, that physical models need to be a little broader and more encompassing. In particular, mind and consciousness are not represented in the best of our scientific models. This is an obvious problem, and it is usually disregarded by saying consciousness is 'just an epiphenomenon' of brain activity. Even to the extent that is true, it clearly does not represent consciousness as we experience it. This short shrift by current science has to be replaced by serious efforts to encompass not only normal conscious experience, but the evidence of high-quality psi research including that generated over more than a decade by the GCP. I like the idea of a 'consciousness field' model, but none exists as yet. Our work is shifting toward deeper analysis, learning more about the structure in the data, ultimately because the empirical findings form the basis for a theoretical understanding.

Iebele: Fritz Popp tried to get to a theoretical framework in his article *Biophysical Aspects of the Psychic Situation*, in which he said that there is a hierarchical order in the variables that describe living organisms. According to Popp, matter is the basis, and then comes energy and then the distribution of energy among matter: entropy. According to Popp, this system describes and introduces potential information too. In the end, he gets to the most highly organized form: consciousness. Popp uses all these variables in a formula, assuming that consciousness is a process transforming actual information into potential information, and vice versa. As an example of using his formula, Popp said that they are able to demonstrate that someone's belief in his own health and the resulting actual health aren't separate phenomena. Said simply, Popp suggested that the relationship between consciousness and matter can be expressed in already-known variables. Even though he focused on complex biological systems, the same relationship between consciousness, information, entropy, energy, and matter could possibly be found in non-biological systems, like electronic machines, and I mean random-event generators, of course. There is considerable evidence now for your assumption that REGs can react to large groups of people who focus their attention or emotions on the same thing.[1] This seems to me to be important knowledge. When this assumption can be supported by an understandable, consistent model, it will probably reach a lot more people than it does now. But we have a long way to go yet.

Roger: Because the data compel thinking about the 'reality' of consciousness as a functional entity that has direct effects in the world, I am dragged into the theoretical domain. It seems that consciousness and information are related on a deep level in the sense that both are made from the gossamer threads of selection and decision, the differences between yes and no, up and down, between the mathematical bits 1 and 0. In this ephemeral world even the distinctions of past and future seem written as potentials, and the difference between potential and actualization becomes material. Mind is made of these subtle movements from virtual to actual, from not at all to powerfully present; mind is the realization of now. Can we distinguish this from information? Is there any way to have existence without information? No, information is structure; it is the patterns that are reality and turn potential into possibility. It creates what otherwise only might have been. This is the power of consciousness waiting to be tapped. Mind matters — it is the creative pinnacle, and it goes all the way down.

Iebele: I think there are many people who recognize this thought process. It comes close to what I mean by a 'natural law of consciousness' in which subjective intuitive and objective empirical thinking converge.

Roger: Since I am basically an empiricist, I don't try to produce a theoretical picture to explain the results of our experiments. But of course I think about it, and one of my favorite sources, David Bohm,

---

1 Coherent Consciousness and Reduced Randomness: Correlations on September 11, Roger Nelson, 2001.

describes virtual information fields in a way that is similar to what you quote from Fritz Popp. Essentially, this view says that there is a universe of potential energies and matter that includes all there is, and is the source of all we perceive, and thus naturally also the foundation of our being and our consciousness. But this still is certainly too remote or fanciful for most people, so I will shift to a more concrete view of what I think is happening at the edges of what we know about consciousness.

Iebele: But isn't that what makes it so interesting? Our power of imagination is, in a way, the only way to obtain insight. People often ask me why I am as involved as I am with these kinds of theoretical considerations. The simple reason is that I like to be able to express how I experience my consciousness. Consciousness and perception seem to be so closely intertwined that each of my perceptions of something 'outside me' evokes something 'inside me.' Sometimes perception seems to be directly linked to being conscious of it, comparable with what you said: consciousness is the realization of now. It works the other way round too, however. If I create something, a thought or an idea manifests in the process, by which consciousness seems to become very concrete. Even quite complex thoughts, like thinking about potentiality and actuality, one can express in form by, for example, developing a process for it, like I do in my work. What fascinates me is that such abstract, complex thoughts can be transferred into an artwork and that people who see the work later understand or sense, more or less, what it is about.

Roger: Art and music by their nature are mentally and emotionally active. Their real existence is not in the material, color, or sound, but in our perception of and reaction to them. This suggests a direct message in the form of a challenge to science, and an inspiration to everyone, that says, "Look at this beauty; listen to this richness. What does the fact of art tell us about the nature of our being?" We *create* something new in every aesthetic production, and in every moment of enjoyment we become different. This isn't conscious, for most of us, but it can be. We can see a path to a more conscious and a more evolved future, and we can see it now. It remains only to accept the possibility, and decide to take the responsibility. The artist's role is to inspire movement in these directions.

Iebele: Certainly, the essential nature of things is far beyond the colors, materials, and sounds. The depth of looking is often strongly determined by the limits of one's own opinions. To get closer to the essential nature of things, one has to be willing to go beyond the external form and, in particular, one has to *dare* to look. The external form can be described objectively to a certain extent and the objective description has been the determining norm with which reality has been approached for a long time. Gradually this view seems to be broadening, so that subjective experiences are being recognized more by the general public, as opposed to only by the art world. Art is seen by many people as an escape from the strict demands of objectivity. In art, it is often said, we can show and recognize personal — and therefore subjective — feelings. The interesting thing is — and I think this is remarkable — that in this time when society directs more and more attention toward the spiritual, art wants to profile itself scientifically. Many artists, art historians, and curators are introducing more and more of an artistic, intellectual formalism, which is exactly what excludes the subjective experience. In other words, the materialistic idea of classical 'old' science still has an important influence, not only in science itself, but obviously in art as well. Thus, I think both science and art need to widen their scope, to prevent themselves getting too remote from the spiritual explorations that many people are engaged in at this moment. That is why I think cooperation is important. Your findings, for example, in the Global Consciousness Project reinforce the idea of connectedness among people, animals, nature, and things. It seems to be self-evident for art to express this, but it is much less self-evident than you think. Perhaps this is because looking for connectedness is also the core of religious and spiritual movements, which are often looked at with suspicion. I think your research is so interesting because it supplies direct, objective instructions to think in terms of connectedness. Connectedness, on whatever level, has been a central theme in all traditional wisdom and artistic expressions all over the world for thousands of years. Obviously every era, including ours, has to find new ways to give this connectedness a place in society. I think that this is exactly art's primary task. It is not simple, because we have a period behind us in which every reference to a spiritual experience was destroyed or ridiculed. That is why I say sometimes that my main work is the emancipation of spirituality.

Roger: That's right. I am often asked where the Project will go, and what its ultimate goal might be. This is the direction or purpose that is most important to me. The future of the Earth, or more particularly, of its layer of living beings, is in trouble now. This is because we have advanced technologically but not socially, and now have powers that threaten our own wellbeing and that of life on this planet because we have not learned, or do not believe, that we are all interconnected and interdependent. The GCP data provide very clear evidence of the interconnection — when we are driven by great events to share thoughts and emotions, the 'needles' move. We see real effects in the physical world that are a function of our shared consciousness. The interconnection is driven by events, but we also show it can be brought into being intentionally, when people organize to share a holiday, or a global musical event, or a worldwide meditation. This implies, obviously, that we are capable of sharing ideas and feelings on a deep, unconscious level, and that this affects the way things are in the world. We don't need to be conscious of this, any more than a neuron needs to be aware of its role in creating our minds. But if ever greater numbers of people come to understand the subtle interaction that is our birthright, it will become part of our lives, and allow us to live to our potential as humans. We are capable of conscious evolution, and it is becoming clear that it is also our responsibility.

Iebele: I don't think we should underestimate the issue of learning to understand to what extent the reality of our body needs a spiritual reality and vice versa,. There seems to be a connection between consciousness and matter, which many people have clearly sensed for a long time. But even people who suggest that our reality is strictly material, and who do not attribute any meaning to consciousness, *survive*. Maybe at the cost of others, but that doesn't matter if one doesn't feel a deeper connectedness with the surroundings. Powers like that, exclusively self-directed, don't develop a deeper insight until it becomes very clear 'how it is.' I definitely include myself in this. I, too, need clarity in order to understand my true responsibility. I'm far from understanding the real interaction between my body and my consciousness, let alone that I understand how I'm connected with others. I don't *know* it, so how *can* I act correctly? What I want to say is that the right knowledge seems to me to be indispensable for the right action. It's easy for me to say that my body and consciousness are one, and I can experience it that way. But I can experience, too, that my body and my consciousness are separate entities. Maybe both are true, depending on the moment. Why do I keep thinking about this over and over again? Probably because the way I was raised and the knowledge I have collected is incomplete, or possibly all wrong. How can I look at myself and my surroundings as if everything is self-evident, if my starting point is an imperfect understanding? To get back to your point: it is not easy to take responsibility for something you don't understand. I don't understand life, and it would be a great deal easier if I did. In my work, I can direct my attention to a framed reality: the relationship between consciousness and matter. I do this because I assume that there is a reality behind everyday reality, and I assume that reality is 'consciousness.' But not until the mystery of this consciousness has opened to me a little, can I be a human being who is a little more complete. This happens in very small steps, while the mystery keeps getting larger with every small step.

Roger: It is not easy to escape the training of a lifetime. Both in our ordinary experiences of touching and smelling the world, and in the classical physics of action and reaction, the case is clear: we can accurately describe the physical world of material and energy, and we can make cars, and chop down trees, and swim in the oceans. We can manipulate the world pretty much as we desire. And so, when we ask deeper questions, or contemplate more subtle qualities, our first instinct is to bring the powerful tools of physics and mathematical formulation to bear. But how do we deal with poetry, with the experience of sky-blue or sunset red? What makes music so emotionally powerful? How do we explain love with our equations? These harder questions are simply not addressed by the 'queen of sciences' even though they are a real and important part of the world we want to understand. It is time to stretch the boundaries to include all there is. This isn't a simple thing to do, but it really is time to accept the difficult task and get on with it.

Science of the Subjective

Conversation with Brenda Dunne and Robert Jahn, Princeton, March 2009

Brenda Dunne is a developmental psychologist and President of the International Consciousness Research Laboratories in Princeton (ICRL), which she established together with Prof. Dr. Robert Jahn. In 1979, Bob and Brenda founded the Princeton Anomalies Engineering Research laboratory (PEAR) at Princeton University, where they did research in consciousness-related anomalies for nearly thirty years. Bob is a highly respected aerospace scientist who served as Dean of Princeton's School of Engineering and Applied Science for fifteen years.

Iebele: The two of you have tried to bring together a great number of disciplines like psychology, mysticism, philosophy, physics, quantum physics, and world religions in your research and publications. You studied phenomena like human/machine anomalies and remote perception for nearly three decades, and established by means of statistical analysis that many inexplicable phenomena probably are not based on coincidence, but instead show significant correlations with our consciousness. One of the reasons we meet each other here in Princeton, is to discuss whether I can improve the way in which I attempt to evoke music and images from consciousness. Thus far I have used the method you used all those years, where you demonstrated that the outcome of a random generator can be deflected from the probable average and shows the possible connection between consciousness and matter. You used statistical evaluation of the numbers that the random generator produced to prove these connections. If a particular output was correlated with the stated intention of a human operator, that was an indication that more than coincidence was at play, something that seems to relate to intentions or emotions in an inexplicable way. I wonder if there are any other ways beside statistical analysis to describe this phenomenon. Statistics is playing with numbers; consciousness, to me, is much more than that.

Bob: Of course there are other ways to deal with consciousness beside the statistical. My problem is, has been, and will probably continue to be that I deal with people who can only be convinced by our data when I point out the statistical results. Everything we mention in our articles, the psychological and metaphysical consequences of our work, for example, will only be taken seriously if we are able to support our results with numbers, with statistical evidence.

Brenda: Numbers and statistics are the language of science, while consciousness is of course much more subtle than numbers, just like you said.

Iebele: Bob said that there are other ways to deal with consciousness. I am curious about those.

Brenda: Bob does not mean scientific or technological methods. If you talk about consciousness it is important to know who your public is. We tune our story to that.

Iebele: My public consists of people who listen to my music, or look at my images. What they want to see and what I want to make is *form*. The way I attain form is by looking for structure. The random generators we use produce 'noise'[1] based on quantum processes. We, you and I, try to find moments in this 'noise' when it deviates from its normal behavior. If that moment coincides with a certain intention or mood we say: you see, it is not mere coincidence, it is more! And that 'more' we then connect with consciousness. The only way I have found so far to find this kind of deviation in noise is by means of statistics[1]. Statistics describes deviations from chance. I can do all kinds of things with it, but how can I explain it to people who want to see or hear "form"? That's why I look for a method to investigate the noise of a random generator in a morphologic way; for image and music are about form, not about numbers. It would be nice if one could say: look, this random generator behaves a certain way and that proves there is activity or rest in the environment. After all, the EEG used in brain research gives these kinds of indications too. Slow brain waves indicate rest; fast waves indicate increased brain activity. I'm looking for something like that by using the quantum noise of a random generator.

---

1 An REG produces digital ones and zeroes. Translated into sound this sounds like noise. Generally speaking, an REG produces an ideal 'white' noise.

Brenda: It may sound a little cryptic, but the method you are looking for is the activity of *consciousness*, I think.

Bob: The task you have taken on is definitely not a simple one. First of all, you want to determine if the signals you receive from a machine, be it an EEG or an REG, correspond with what we call consciousness. Both an EEG signal and a deviation in a REG may indicate a certain change, but the meaning of that change is unknown. A fast EEG may mean all kinds of things relating to our consciousness or our feelings. The brain activity may be increased because you read a love letter or because you just received the divorce papers from your wife. That is the first problem: EEGs or REGs only measure the quantitative aspects of a phenomenon, not the qualitative ones. But there is another issue. The new concepts studied in science nowadays are things like chaos, complexity, and non-linear systems. There is more and more evidence for physical systems that don't function according to a well-defined order. These are systems that can't be replicated. They are not deterministic and not falsifiable. They are not even linear. These kinds of systems can be started by a well-defined set of conditions and then they do something. If the same system is started again in exactly the same way, it does something completely different. It is still unclear how we have to deal with this in the present way of scientific thinking. Science has always been deterministic, and now we have discovered systems that don't seem to be deterministic.

Iebele: If there is a chaotic system that at any moment develops into a certain form and that form keeps changing, with the initial parameters staying the same, it could be a sensor for changes in consciousness.

Bob: Absolutely. That could well be. But much work needs to be done before we can apply these systems that way, if it is at all possible. We are just at the point where we have learned to know these phenomena. When researchers got in touch with these complex systems for the first time — and that was just a few decades ago — they first tried to adjust scientific models and concepts to them. That always happens in science when something is found that deviates from the existing model. The common response is to adjust the current view in such a way that the new phenomenon will fit into it, instead of investigating what is wrong with the current view. We have seen this happen again and again in history. The big debate about the heliocentric and geocentric solar system is just one example out of many. Copernicus and Galileo looked through their telescopes, described what they saw and derived a model from it in which the sun is the center of our solar system. And they were right; at least that is what we think now. But the establishment tried as hard as it could to describe the movements of the planets observed by Copernicus and Galileo as if the Earth was the center of the solar system. This was not wrong in the strict sense of the word, because it is possible to calculate the movements of the planets based on cycloids with the Earth as the center. But why would one do that if a simpler and more elegant way is available by using ellipses? How many people know what a cycloid is? It is just much simpler to take the sun as the center of the universe. At this point in history exactly the same is happening. We are confronted with the question of what to do with the observation of complex chaotic systems, and most of all, how to fit these systems in the scientific frameworks of the 20th and 21st centuries. The latest discoveries are explained by all kinds of bizarre mechanistic theories. And that doesn't seem to work well. It is getting too complicated.

Brenda: Like string theories with 36 dimensions, which nobody can conceive of in logical terms.

Bob: It is not a matter of these theories being right or wrong. It is about what we think is right and what isn't. Researchers are caught in string theories because they work, to a certain extent. The problem with these theories is that they are so grotesquely complicated. One gets caught in an enormous spiral of knowledge and mathematics that it is no longer a facile representation of the phenomena that one wants to explain.

Brenda: If one has to study for thirty years to understand the language and mathematics of a theory, the representation of reality one has found can hardly be called broadly useful.

Bob: All those complicated theories are like repairing a watch with boxing gloves on. And exactly the same is true for non-linear complex systems. Can we understand our consciousness better from all the books that have been filled about these non-linear systems, because consciousness may be non-linear? Maybe. Maybe they will give you an answer. But it could take another century before you have found that answer.

And the question remains whether it will be the "right" answer.

Brenda: You have the same problem in your work, of course. You have collected a lot of knowledge which you now use in your art and music. The explanation of how you make your work is too complicated for most people because they did not all study consciousness and matter like you did. That is why you make images that show what you found when you did the research. Those images and music of yours are a simplified version of your knowledge. They represent the more complex, deeper considerations you have, and that is why someone who sees your work can say: "I understand what this artist wants to express."

Iebele: I want to find a way to express a certain idea; an assumption that our reality and our consciousness are inextricably connected. Such an assumption doesn't have a form yet, it is only an idea, a thought. To concretize such an idea one needs a technique. When a painter has the idea that he can better express himself if he is able to depict the layers of reality by transparent means, he needs a technique that makes this possible. He discovers, for example, that he can dilute oil paint with a transparent agent and by doing that he can apply colors layer by layer. Such a technique, glazing, enables the painter to create deep, lively colors. I feel like a painter who is looking for the right technique. How can I transform the observation of my consciousness into form? This is of course a very abstract goal, but it exists very concretely in me and in the society too, as far as I understand society at any rate. One way to make the interaction between consciousness and the world tangible is to develop a technique or method that gives rise to visible forms from the immaterial domain of consciousness. Your method of demonstrating the relationship between consciousness and matter statistically reasonably concretizes what I mean. I have used this very method to create images and music, and the result is fairly close to what I want to reach. Maybe the images I make speak for themselves. There are people who say: "I understand exactly what that guy wants to say with his work." But there are still many more people who may *sense* it, but still ask me how I create my work exactly. I can try to explain it, but by far not everyone understands the technique. I can also try to make work that is even clearer. But in order for this to be possible the technique needs to improve; it has to become more easily understandable intuitively.

Bob: That is what Brenda meant to say: that is what *you* can do. As scientists we are bound to our culture. The task of expressing consciousness in numbers is almost undoable, and physics simply works with numbers. You work in a different culture. You can express things in images and music that we cannot describe with our tools. We don't have any tools but statistics to say: "Something is the matter with a reality that doesn't agree with the laws of physics, and it seems to be associated with consciousness." That is all we can do, and we have been doing it for over thirty years. We've tried to prove scientifically the fact that there is more than a mechanical, materialistic reality. And the evidence exists. We have contributed to it. That is our field, and it inspires you obviously. It is your field to *show* reality.

Brenda: When we wrote *Margins of Reality* in 1978 we said to each other: "Good heavens, this subject is so broad, for whom exactly are we writing it? Are we writing for scientists, philosophers, mystics, or artists?" In the end we decided to write a separate chapter for each group. Every chapter got a different perspective and a separate introduction and was written for a certain target group. We wrote about the history of science, about quantum mechanics, biology, and so on. That way we were able to put the results of our research in a different context in each chapter.

Iebele: Art and music of course have most of all an 'emotional' or 'feeling' value. But art is cognitive as well; it does not come forth from 'feeling' alone but also from thinking. Feeling and knowledge both are forms of information. The latest models of science speak about information. If methods existed to measure 'consciousness information,' one could repeat a subjective experience and register it more or less objectively. That could be very interesting from an artistic viewpoint, if possible at all.

Bob: Some models claim that this *could* be done. But if one asks if consciousness and subjective experiences can be described by numbers, the answer is: no, not yet. What we *can* do, however, is describe our experiences semi-quantitatively. If you ask me how I feel today and I answer "Better than yesterday," I have, in my opinion, given a clear answer. And if you then ask, which is what science does:

"Are you sure this is the right answer? Can you prove that you feel better than yesterday?" you are asking for trouble. Questions and answers concerning our consciousness are forms of semi-quantitative information. One can judge the quality of these questions and the answers by seeing if they are simple and direct. Does the question describe the information that you want to transfer?

Iebele: What you are saying implicitly is that 'information fields,' a popular concept, cannot be compared with power fields or energy fields. It is possible to attribute a value, a number, to power or energy, but not to subjective information. I think that is an important issue because in the popular opinion our consciousness is active as a field. In principle, one could tune to that field to receive or give information. Information in physics seems to be a concrete quantity. But for me the concept of information is just as ungraspable as that of consciousness. They seem to be two different words for the same thing, don't they?

Brenda: In physics, fields, power fields, or energy fields are subsets of information.

Bob: Let's say we are going to an opera tonight. Will we enjoy it? Will it appeal to us on an emotional level? And if so, what does that have to do with the musical notes in the score? And how do these notes relate to the man or woman who plays the oboe tonight? There are so many dimensions to a satisfying experience. One can study the score and say: "That should sound fantastic!" Maybe the oboist looks at the organization or the set and thinks: "This is a fantastic production!" Or one goes to the opera as a member of the public, to look and simply listen to it.

Brenda: Suppose all three of us read the same book. We see the same letters, the same images. But we read the book from our own different backgrounds. Bob interprets the book as a physicist, I interpret it as a psychologist, and you interpret it as an artist. That is the subjective dimension, while the physical information is the same.

Iebele: All right, but isn't information a concrete variable at the same time? Does it really exist as a workable concept for you in your professions as psychologist and physicist?

Bob: Of course, information is a valid variable in physics.

Brenda: The advantage of information over variables like mass and energy is that information has a subjective dimension as well. Information is what you think it is. This coffee mug for example. I use it to drink coffee from it. For someone else it is an ashtray.

Iebele: But the way you say it now, information is nothing else but a collection of metaphors.

Bob: In the description of reality we use *nothing but* metaphors.

Iebele: So is that your whole point?

Bob: My point is that we have nothing but metaphors: information, gravity, electromagnetic fields. These are all metaphors that we have created to grasp what we think is happening on this planet. Nobody has ever brought an electromagnetic field home from work for dinner. But that does not make it a less important instrument for learning to understand what is happening in our reality. The same is true for information. It is a good metaphor.

Brenda: Two hundred years ago electromagnetism was regarded as pure magic. Until someone stood up who was able to describe it in a model. Then it was no longer magic, because we were able to predict what would happen.

Iebele: And do you think such a predicting description of information may ever appear?

Brenda: So far nobody has proposed a model that can incorporate the subjective aspects of information.

Bob: We need words, a conceptual vocabulary to enable us to describe subjective information quantitatively. We are not there yet. So far we only utilize a semi-quantitative vocabulary. I can say I love Brenda *a lot*. But I can't say I love Brenda *17.8*. Our vocabulary doesn't work like that. A random generator that responds to my love will give a number, but such a number isn't a particularly satisfactory, let alone a complete way to describe information or consciousness.

Brenda: Using numbers is just a way to reach a more or less precise consensus about the length of a meter.

Bob: There are people who are busy with nothing else but determining an extremely precise definition of a meter. But whichever measuring rod they use, there is none without a scratch. And the measuring tools they use are so advanced that even the wave length of light sources in the measuring room influences the length of a meter.

Brenda: And if one studies the literature, big problems appear to arise in determining the length of a meter, because the cosmological constants tend to change. Even the speed of light turns out to change depending on the moment when one looks at it. The speed of light changes just a tiny little bit, but if one worries about that kind of thing, it may cause sleepless nights.

Iebele: Everyone tries in his own way to get a grip on reality of course, but sooner or later one gets to a point where it turns out that nothing remains. That is how our life goes by. Why wouldn't those so-called constants be changeable? I see this as the bridge between the exact, rational thinking and emotional processes. It may say something about the denseness of consciousness that the physical reality tends to change less than our consciousness. The denser and more compact things are, the less they change. That's why I think about consciousness as a light reality. I experience the physical reality as much denser. It is comparable to ice, water, and steam. Ice is firm, it is almost impossible to change its form. Water is much more fluid, and steam even more so. Water and steam may take on all forms, while ice more or less remains the same form. Even if this is the case, the form of a chunk of ice came from water. Ice is literally a solidified form of water. I can imagine that our consciousness is able to take all kinds of forms *because* of its lightness, and that the physical, more dense reality, may be a solidified reproduction of our consciousness at a certain moment. Our physical reality may be the result of the millions of years during which our consciousness has developed. I wonder why we experience our dreams as less real that the reality in our waking consciousness. We direct our attention often to the physical reality, and that reality is rather unruly. It doesn't always do what we want. In our fantasy we can create every reality we wish. Sometimes I think that our experience of reality just isn't quite adequate. Why is all of it so *firm and solid* here? We were just talking about metaphors. One may wonder if everything we observe is nothing but an accumulation of metaphors: immaterial, conceptual tissues of our consciousness. If that is true, one can ask fundamental questions about reality. Reality may be nothing else than our consciousness of it. One can continue and reach the point that everything is an illusion, including that which seems to be firm and solid. The table here only exists because we have the same consciousness experience about it.

Brenda: If our reality is indeed defined by waves and quantum processes, if this reality has an infinite potential regarding its forms of appearance, and if we know that all matter around us is in fact built from empty space, thinking on that level, how is it possible that this table feels so solid when I bump into it? I think that is the underlying question we are concerned about. Why can't I stick my hand through a wall? Is that because of my consciousness or is it because of a 'real' reality? I think at some level we choose to live in a physical body in a physical world. We accept that metaphors of reality limit us to a more or less solid reality at the same time. And this reality seems to behave according to certain patterns. But these patterns are metaphors as well. One lives within the circle of one's own consciousness. If one starts to use different metaphors by oneself, or change their meaning, the world changes for us. But only when other people do the same, only when they too attribute the same meaning to our metaphors, it 'really' changes. Only then it is 'objective.' We just try to come to agreement among each other about how we define reality, and it is mostly different for everyone, and yet the same in some aspects. That's why science is so fond of numbers. It is easy to agree with each other about numbers. A meter is a meter. But the experiences people have that can't be measured are hard to process in science. And that is what we want to say: the subjective experience is the key to our consciousness. The objective, deterministic, quantitative description of reality obscures subjective experience. *All of it* is consciousness.

Iebele: I was born in a world which, probably as I got older, I experienced more and more as fixed. My life as a physical being limits to a certain extent my freedom to move. In my dreams I move around much more freely than in daily life. Because of my dreams and imagination I know there is more than the fixed reality.

Bob: Whether this pleases us or not, we are limited in our existence to a certain extent because our life has developed in history into a form in which causality plays an explicit role. What you are looking for, and I think this is a *dream reality*, is still a living reality.

Very little attention is paid tothis reality of our consciousness, the dreams and the imagination. It is dying a slow death, if we don't pay attention to it. The challenge is therefore to investigate in which measure the spiritual dimension can be brought to the public dialogue. To do this one needs to be able to describe this dimension in a tangible way because that is the norm. But is that possible? We have discovered so far that the spiritual dimensions influence the world too, but these effects are very small. At least in the way we have measured them. That is why they are not yet very convincing for science.

Iebele: Nevertheless these effects are taken seriously, particularly in all kinds of spiritual movements. In these movements I see a certain form of activism. Your research and publications have an activist 'spirit' like this as well. The society as we know it now is a construction of technology, models, laws, and rules that determine our daily life considerably. I think that strict deterministic thinking slowly will loosen up, because many people draw the sense of their life from realities which are less 'testable,' which spring forth from feelings, dreams, imagination, love, compassion, and empathy. These realities claim their place too. Some present social movements resemble the theosophical movement in the beginning of the 20th century. Consciousness plays a big role in both of them, and the need occurs in both to give spiritual thinking a place in thinking about society. I think that this need has always existed, but nowadays its presence is clearly recognizable, as it seems to differ so much from purely technological thinking.

Bob: Well, you call this activism, but am I wrong when I say that all of the really great art aims at the transcendent? In our terms I would say that the artist sees the wavelike character of things, the spiritual. I think the artist's task is to explore the soul and represent it. Isn't that what the *Mona Lisa* is really about? Often I don't understand modern art, but I presume that artists nowadays try to say something that can't be expressed with a different medium or genre.

Iebele: That is, of course, the problem one bumps into in art: there is no determined general standard with which one can interpret the value or meaning of an artwork. I don't know if this is has always been so or if it is specifically true for this time, but I think people have always sought for universal concepts in history, and that an art work, a book, or piece of music sometimes can express something universal. But this always happens in the language and symbols of the time. The recognition of life's mystery lies at the basis of universal understanding, separate from the language and symbols, and the recognition of that mystery has moved to the background in our time because of the expectation that science, by thinking strictly causally and deterministically, would be able to answer all questions. I don't think all questions can be answered, and certainly not from only one point of view.

Bob: If you look at Aboriginal cultures, you see that they maintain a better balance between experience and its representation in language. I mean that we live for close to a hundred percent in a tangible, causal, determinable reality. Only a small fraction of our reality exists in the spiritual dimension.

Iebele: That is why I am interested in the older wisdom traditions. Mysticism looks for the origin and the experiencing of life's mystery. That dimension is very different from the purely material one. The big challenge has always been, however, how to relate to one's origin, which we can never know completely simply because it surpasses the individual comprehension. I think this is where the concept of God comes from. God is in esotericism nothing but a metaphor for 'all that is.' Knowing that, we can't completely comprehend the extent of the universe on an individual level, the first and possibly the only step we can take as humans in this research is to study our immediate environment. The major difference I see between the empirical sciences and mysticism is that the latter one, in addition to our cosmos, also involves the far-reaching scope of our own consciousness.

Brenda: One can go back in history and notice that spirituality has always played a role. The art by cave drawers was spiritual. They drew a reindeer because they wanted to hunt the animal, so they evoked the reindeer's spirit by making its physical representation on a cave wall. And when the artist did his work well, it worked. The hunters went to hunt and the reindeer was there! One finds the same principle in ancient architecture. People made constructions especially designed to evoke a specific state of mind. On entering such a building one experiences a spiritual dimension. That is what you also try to do in your work. The work itself is the metaphor, it refers to a spiritual experience, and at the same time it evokes it, just like such a building.

Bob: You mentioned the word *God*. I think we can only perceive a small part of what we call the 'Source.' Depending on the filters we put up between ourselves and the Source we get a certain experience. These filters are necessary because otherwise we would be buried by a cacophony of impressions. I think what you are working on is a way to change the set-up of these filters of reality a little differently, to make it possible to receive different signals from the Source. One can establish such a filter for all kinds of things, but I don't think we can choose a setting which enables one to perceive everything at once, or to fix everything which is. The Source, that original sense of omnipresence, is a lively, flowering, humming *confusion*. Some way or another there is a 'container' which contains all potential realities. We exchange information with a small part of this container by looking through our own filters. That is how we bring about structure in what we perceive. What I want to say is: *everything is there*. The implicit question you pose is, do the very small deviations we have found in the physical world under influence of consciousness, point to this 'everything there is.'

Brenda: What we need is a language with which we can describe this. Science speaks this language hardly or not at all. What we have seen is that our results are connected to subjective experiences: the significant outcomes of our random generators correlate with conscious intentions, but the nature of these intentions may vary per person. For example, the random generators seem to respond differently to men and women. This is the pitfall: two concepts that have difficulty finding a place in science: subjective experience and acausal processes. The reaction of a random generator to the changing consciousness of an experimental operator is unexplainable since it is essentially a subjective phenomenon. That is our problem. We investigate things that bring the fundamental assumptions of current scientific thinking into dispute. Our findings are not causal, and on top of that they are subjective.

Bob: What you want to do is to show aspects of consciousness and the unexplainable mystery. Just like us, you are looking for a way to be as convincing as possible. I think you, being an artist, can do that better than we, being scientists. We have received certain tools, certain training. We have been taught concepts, rules, and laws. Everything in our training, apart from a few exceptions, was directed at our becoming very good materialists. With this conditioning, our very precise instruments, which point exclusively at quantitative perceptions are in fact doomed to fail before we even try to investigate the small deviations that consciousness introduces into the world. If we want to continue with our research within the culture of science, we will need to depart from the usual tools, techniques, and convictions. That is the only way for us to show that there is something not quite right with causal thinking. It would be very pleasing, of course, if we were able to make the foundation of causal thinking crack. If we could part the Red Sea once more, or if we could fly…. But what *we* have been able to do until now at least shows that when one practices science according to the rules of the game, one encounters things that don't fit in. There are things associated with the subjective dimensions of our consciousness that will remain unexplainable as long as the rules of science preclude those dimensions.

Iebele: That's why you have written *Change the Rules*.

Bob: Exactly.

Iebele: A rather technological idea that is widely used in mainstream media are *cyborgs*; a rather old idea actually. They are those beings half machine, half human, you can find in science fiction. People may always have been cyborgs in a certain sense, because they hardly seem to be able to survive without tools. I bring this up because technology on the one hand can widen the perception of reality, but on the other hand narrow it. What you just said is clearly a plea to think not only in terms of technology, but also in terms of poetry, music, and art. Even though this is the case, if one puts glasses on, one sees the world a lot clearer. That is technology too. One can imagine that, next to the development of one's own consciousness, a technology might be developed that raises consciousness by making truths visible that otherwise would have remained invisible.

Bob: You were talking about dreaming earlier. Dreaming is an unintentional resetting of filters: we receive information during our dreams from a source that is hardly accessible to us while we are awake. That is like opening a shutter that was closed, developing a whole new series of impressions. Is what you want to reach something like that?

Iebele: Yes, something like that. Your research makes clear on a very small scale that part of such a reality can penetrate the physical reality. And you use machines for it. That way you show that realities that existed only in the immaterial domain before, somehow can also be detected in the everyday world, although to a lesser degree. Look, whether one's technique is painting, silk-screen, or designing computer games, every artist uses tools. It is interesting to see if new tools are really able to evoke new experiences. Those who use new media in arts try to do just that, of course. I am specifically looking for how to concretize the ungraspable relationship between consciousness, perceptions, and reality. I succeed only partially with the existing technologies. The random generators and EEG come closest. The best technology in the whole world is of course our own body, but one wants to create something oneself once in a while. When I don't create anything I feel unsatisfied. I don't know where the urge to create something comes from, but it is there, so let me use it to pose my big questions. Why am I here? Why am I aware of my being alive? What is the meaning of everything I see?

Brenda: Your music obviously brings together consciousness, perception, and reality. It widens the dimensions of consciousness, even if it uses modern technology, doesn't it? You are already posing these questions and processing them in your work.

Bob: The problem Iebele sees is that though the machines we have at our disposal have the potential to reach a widened consciousness, they were originally designed to reach just the opposite. Isn't that true? All these machines communicate in current language and current images. They distribute information of the same general character that everyone already knows. Electronics have not been developed to do what Iebele wants to do with it. Games, television, and that kind of stuff have not been developed to investigate different consciousness levels. They do just the opposite; they bring people even deeper into a material world.

Iebele: And yet I think that the invention of the radio or the telephone can very well be seen as a technological equivalent of telepathy. All one has to do is to strike a few a number keys and one is in touch with someone else, wherever one is on the planet. I once had a conversation with someone to whom I tried to explain why I think the noise of a REG is so interesting. In the end I reached a rather 'exotic' aspect of my fascination: we have radio, TV, and internet to communicate with one another. All of that is communication at a level we know well; we send and receive speech and images in a *certain* way. This way of communication could also be different. Suppose we can communicate on a non-local level, past the limits of space and time? The interaction between consciousness and REGs is supposed to be non-local. It may be far-fetched, but perhaps we are potentially even able to communicate this way beyond the limits of life and death. My father has been dead for almost forty years, and I often talk with him in my mind. I'm not saying I talk with *him*, but I talk then with *someone*, maybe myself. How would it be to get him on the phone? The Akasha chronicles that are mentioned in theosophy, store information from all times of the cosmos and the people in an immaterial way. The information of the dead likewise. Comparable to what Bob called the 'Source.'

Brenda: The idea that 'white noise' is a carrier of information that we can't normally receive is not strange at all. Actually it is a common phenomenon. We have documentation about it, and I have experienced it during a very simple experiment when I listened to noise. I heard voices and someone else did too.

Bob: Current technology is not designed to receive such information or to transmit it. What comes closest is what Psyleron tries to do with Syntext[2] technology. They try, just like you, to evoke subtle forms of information by means of technology. There are, however, not many people who do this because there is hardly any 'supporting power' for technology like this. Someone who buys a cell phone generally speaking doesn't want to hear random messages or see images that he normally doesn't see.

Iebele: I do.

Bob: I agree with you that it must be possible. But it is an open field, because there are not many people who choose this option.

Brenda: We humans have limited senses. We have been able to broaden our perception with glasses, telescopes, microscopes, hearing aids, x-ray cameras, you name it. We are most dependent of the visual dimension,

---

2 Syntext is a message system based on REGs, that sends selected messages at seemingly random moments. The experience of the users is that the random messages often turn out to be meaningful and timely.

and this dimension is, neurologically speaking, closely linked with language, i.e. language and image are intertwined. Seeing has more or less the same structure as thinking in language. One has to experience a very strong change in one's consciousness for the experience of reality to change. Such a change may happen during meditation, by taking chemical agents, or during sleep. In synesthesia, what happens is that sense impressions melt into each other, because thinking and language are no longer in between. Colors become scents, tastes become sounds. That is a form of a widened consciousness that is hard to express in language because language knows mostly metaphors in the form of images. That's why I think what you want to reach would be easier to do by music than in images. Music is less fixed into rational, linguistic structures.

Bob: You do comparable things with your music. It is diverted from other sensors than the auditory. You use rational schemes and you accept intuitive impulses to *think up* your music. And only then you translate it into music. That is totally different from making music with your 'ears.' Therefore I think your music links consciousness, perception, and reality.

Brenda: I think our language is able to use the information of thinking and the senses in all kinds of contexts. By combining thinking with seeing in your work, you realize a 'cross wire.' That's why it evokes a 'lively' sensation. Years ago I attended a sandpainting ceremony, where the monks chanted. I was so touched that I purchased a recording, and when I listened to that at home I noticed that I felt the different sounds also in different parts of my body. I experience the same with your CD, *13 Moon Music*, I can *feel* that music. I have listened to it many times in the past few weeks, and it strikes me as an art form that surpasses one single modality. It is not just an auditory experience, it is more than that. Some frequencies I feel in my throat, others in my hands, and others again in my abdomen. Sound is perceived as a physiological response by your music. It appeals to several sense filters at the same time. And that is how you *thought it up*: you want to evoke an experience of timelessness by using cyclical patterns and all kinds of different concepts having to do with time. And in your music these concepts work! I sometimes suffer from insomnia, but this music makes me sleep excellently. The relaxation that your music provides is another response, on yet another level. That makes your work artistic. Our problem as scientists is that we can't disconnect the importance of the subjective experience from objective reality. One can learn to understand the world better by trying to see the whole picture. It isn't only hearing, it isn't only seeing, it isn't only feeling, it isn't only smelling and tasting, it isn't only thinking, and the world certainly doesn't exist of numbers only. It is all these things together which constitute how we experience the world. *How* we experience something that *is* how it is. I feel your music in my body. Someone else may not, but I do, and someone else's experience does not change that.

Iebele: We listen to a recording of a musical instrument guided by an REG. The intention of this instrument is to react to the changes in consciousness of the one who is listening to it. The music is therefore never the same. I often use this instrument during lectures, but I also experiment with it in my studio. The instrument works rather well with large groups. Usually people feel a heightened sense of togetherness. In this recording the subject was someone who visited the studio for therapeutical reasons. It was a weakened woman who hoped the music would make her feel better. Luckily, I recorded this music session because what happened was incredible. The woman felt a lot better for weeks after the session. I don't know if this was caused by the music or by the suggestion; I'd rather refrain from a pronouncement about that, but the music produced during the session was really magnificent. Because the woman expected so much from the music, the interaction between her and the instrument may have become so powerful, that even when we listen to it again we feel something of the vulnerability, the longing for rest and the love of this woman sounding through the notes.[3] Isn't that miraculous?

Bob: Do you see what happens here? He (the dog) notices that something sublime, something important is happening here. He has only a few ways to express himself to me. And what does he do? He presses himself to me as firmly as he can. Do you have a dog?

Iebele: Yes. A dog, a cat, a wife, and a son.

---

3 The photo on the next page shows the studio with instruments (REG) generating the music.

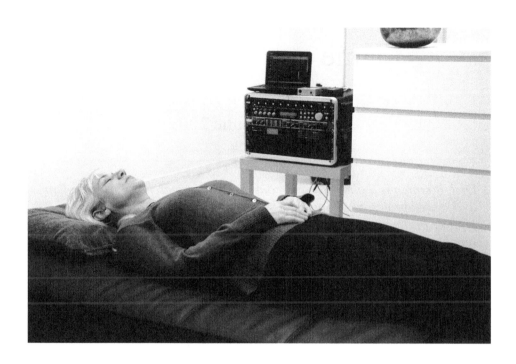

Time and Causality

Conversation with Dick Bierman
Amsterdam, June 2009

Dick Bierman is a physicist and consciousness researcher in Amsterdam and retired professor of Special Experiences in Utrecht. Dick is a pioneer in the research of psychokinesis, which is the discipline that involves bringing matter into motion exclusively by the influence of the psyche. Dick helped me to develop the technique which I use in my work but, above all, he has helped me to become familiar with the basic principles of parapsychological research.

Iebele: When I started the project *Mind over Matter*, the first experiment I had in mind was to try and make a ball on a monitor smaller or bigger, just by wanting it. I imagined a room full of people who were all trying to make the ball bigger.[1] What I found so magical about that idea was that the people in the room wouldn't be connected in any way with the computer that projected the ball on the wall. If something like that were to work, it would make manifest some of the mystery of consciousness; a creative aspect of consciousness would become visible about which traditional wisdom has talked for thousands of years. And of course I didn't just want to project balls; I wanted to use the same idea in my music and images. I was particularly inspired to do experiments like this because this phenomenon has successfully been studied in scientific research. You warned me right away when I started my own research, however, that I might be successful finding mind-matter correlations the first time, but that I should better forget about successfully performing artistic experiments like this in a room full of people. You turned out to be right, although I found some of the magic that I was looking for.

---

1 This experiment has been carried out on a small scale. My son and I tried evening after evening to change the size of such a ball on the monitor. Often with success; my son, especially, was good at it and even better when he smiled.

Dick: One psychokinesis researcher observes a marginal effect with random number generators, an other scores a somewhat stronger effect, and a third one finds nothing at all. Some 800 experiments together show that matter seems to behave in accordance with the intentions of the operator or the subject. Therefore, there is a remarkable correlation between what the subject 'wants' and the behavior of an electric coin-throwing machine. Will and free will are concepts which are heatedly discussed in cognitive psychology. There is a school of thought that doesn't attribute a causal function to our consciousness. In that model, consciousness is an epiphenomenon: the decision you make has already been 'decided' by your brain and your 'I' has no influence on it whatsoever. This standpoint arises from the experiments by Benjamin Libet. Libet himself interpreted his experiments differently, by the way, but the majority of psychologists think that experiencing a mental moment of 'wanting' is nonsense. It has already happened because the brain is always ahead of that experience. The results of experiments with random number generators have a direct relevance for this discussion. In such an experiment, you tell the subject, just as you had in mind, that he or she has to 'want' something, namely to influence the size of a ball. The person tries to want that — which is a mental action — and the matter follows later somehow or other. Such experiments produce firm results, allowing me to say that the will really can influence the world; it's not just an epiphenomenon. Free will exists. That is of course what we experience, too. I have always felt uneasy when science says that something we continuously experience is nonsense. On the other hand, I know we have limitations, so we can't always predict how nature works in its totality.

Iebele: The signal of random number generators is produced very subtly by means of quantum mechanical processes. When I started to use these machines, I thought that the subtlety of this process would make it sensitive to changes in consciousness. I selected the REG I use because its principle is reasonably easy to explain. This REG works with photons and a semi-permeable mirror. Every photon has to make a choice at the mirror: being reflected or passing through the mirror. One cannot predict how one single photon will behave, but one can predict that, on average, one half of the photons will be reflected and the other half will pass through.

Dick: Yes, the fundamental point is that one cannot predict how one single photon will behave. Quantum events are chance events. An essential assumption in the quantum theory is that quantum events are by definition probabilistic, and what will happen in one single happening can't be predicted or calculated. One can predict, however, what will happen, on average, if one takes hundreds of events.

Iebele: It's known that, on average, half of the photons will pass through the mirror in the REG. If you have the intention to change this chance, and if that really happens, one may say there is a connection between consciousness and a physical system. This physical system in our case is a quantum physical system. When I started with my experiments I thought that quantum physical systems were used to research psychokinesis because it's relatively easy to influence them.

Dick: Parapsychology did not start to look at random number generators that use quantum processes with the idea that those would be the easiest processes to influence. No, the reason is, that it is a dependable probabilistic process. A second reason for me to use random processes is my interest in seemingly random processes in the brain. I had an inkling that this was linked to creativity, for example. It is still unclear where the neuronal activity in the brain comes from. Most of the time they are firing at a low level, but they can also spike at totally incomprehensible moments. Transformed into sound, that sounds like noise. That process is completely random, we think, for if we look at the distribution of the signal we measure, it looks completely random. It seemed to me that at that level — in the noise of the brain — paranormal processes, like telepathy and clairvoyance, play a role as well.

Iebele: During a telepathic experience, the passage of time as well as cause and effect seem to be reversed. You call that retrocausality. You also say that psychokinesis is in fact presentiment, and that a conscious intention that manifests itself in actuality is a presentiment of a situation that is going to happen. You propose a theory[2] in which you speak about time symmetry and coherence. As far as I understand it,

---

2 Dick J. Bierman, New developments in Presentiment Research or The nature of *Time. Frontier Science*, CTEC (Center for Transdisciplinary Studies on Consciousness), Joaquim Fernandes (Ed.), Universidade Fernando Pessoa Press, Porto, 2002.

this theory suggests that because of a shortage of 'coherent absorbers', the experience of future sensations is so rare that we believe it to be impossible, while a negative time *can* be used, mathematically seen, in laws of nature. I find it interesting that you try to accommodate psychokinesis and telepathy within an existing model. Presentiment could perhaps be explained physically, if there were sufficient 'coherent absorbers' to check this phenomenon empirically. In that case, we are actually talking about a physical model that makes a reasonable case for perception in the past or in the future.

Dick: When I talk about retrocausal effects like presentiments, I mean in the first place emotional or 'time-symmetric' cognitive effects. When I realized that when time goes backwards, thermodynamics go the wrong way as well, I also saw there is a natural development from a random system towards a structured system. The development in normal thermodynamics is that the system is getting more and more random. It loses information. But if the system goes back in time, it is exactly the opposite; you get more and more information, just like in your experiments when structures form of a series of flowers. You could explain the structure that arises as a result of a deviation from chance by letting the time run backward. But the time-symmetry model is of a very qualitative nature, and what I hope is to get a mathematical description of it. We have to realize that the most fundamental problem of the time-symmetry model is that something going back in time could also be the cause of a forward wave of events. Something appears in the present that actually comes from the future, but that can, of course, create something in the future again, which can then create a wave backward and this can go on and on endlessly. The only way to get out of it is to insert a set of comparisons which, in the end, generates the correct solution from the back-and-forth movement among past, future, and present. A mathematical example is the transactional interpretation of quantum physics, in which the future and the past 'negotiate the present.' During some sort of 'handshake' they conclude: "This is how it should be now." This has been worked out mathematically and now I want to try to use it in my model, but until then it remains a bit of nonsense.

Iebele: Nonsense? You arrived at this model from what you have observed in your studies that people had felt, seen, or experienced something that apparently did indeed happen later on.

Dick: I base the model on experiments I did in the area of presentiment, which I believe is part of intuition. I showed emotional and neutral images in a random order. After seeing emotional pictures, people get more excited than with neutral pictures. What I found was that, on average, the subjects became more excited *right before* seeing the emotional pictures than they did with the neutral pictures. One of the most emotional pictures was of a kitten that had been run over and killed and was hard to recognize. The subjects had two experiences; first they saw a lot of blood and after a few seconds it dawned on them it was a kitten. What I noticed is that the subjects' bodies gave an emotional response twice, also *before they saw this image*. There is thus a certain symmetry in the response around the moment of presenting the 'run-over kitten.' This symmetry is not perfectly mirrored, however, for the simple reason that emotional responses rise fast and fall slowly. The small peaks before the stimulus have that too. It is not the *physical* process, therefore, which is reflected in time but the *emotional* process. The physical response seems to go in a normal forward direction, while the emotional response seems to go back in time as well.

Iebele: This makes me think of the way people experience dreams, memories, and emotions. In that 'reality' of consciousness, time seems to have all kinds of curvatures, which make moving in time in both directions uncomplicated. If we project the reality of consciousness into what is happening now, the now moment, consciousness seems to be caught in linear time, while consciousness in its own movement is completely free in its choice to create future situations or to reconstruct the past. As soon as one steps out of the current situation, as a conscious choice, the 'dream reality' or 'memory' still has reality value for consciousness as an experiential fact; the only difference being, it doesn't have material manifestation.

Dick: That is just like a mystical reality. If one steps out of time, all kinds of things happen, of course. There are two possible models for the mystical experience. The first model assumes that there is an oxygen shortage in the brain during a mystical experience, or that something goes wrong with the wiring or whatever. The other model assumes that something goes 'wrong' with time and space, and I think this last one is not unlikely. I think the first model is not to be ruled out altogether either, because both cases may occur. What you said about escaping time is a beautiful metaphor for a mystical experience. Yes, a mystical experience is in fact escaping time.

Iebele: I often think also about the question of what physics would be without time. What is interesting about this question, in my opinion, is that we are still talking about a description of a tangible reality, but then seen from a non-linear time perspective, like in our dreams, fantasies, and feeling experiences. Suppose you decided not to let time play a role in the description of observations, there still may be 'movement,' but having a different variable than time; maybe a variable that we don't know yet, that we haven't discovered yet.

Dick: In relativity theory, there is something like 'block universe.' It is always there, future and past already exist, but we travel through it, so to speak. That is one interpretation, but your remark makes me think even more of the time I worked for *Interval*, a think tank in Silicon Valley, where they wanted to develop quantum computers. A mathematician who worked there, Tom Etter, developed a primal theory from which, according to him, quantum physics and relativity theory could be deduced. The most interesting was that this theory didn't include time. The theory involved relationships, just like in a network in which we, as nodes, have relationships with other nodes in the network. This relationship was not causal in this theory; it didn't matter if something was or wasn't causal. The relationship was one between nodes, and if you developed it further, quantum physics appeared. I don't think this is true, for if it had been true, the guy would have become world famous years ago, but it has made me think about what a 'prototheory' should look like. Every physicist understands that we are not there yet by far, and that the more we try to bring all material processes together into one model, the more the problems are actually increasing. For this reason, I wouldn't be surprised if the 'prototheory' didn't contain time, or contained it in a very different way.

Iebele: What fascinates me is that consciousness may be described as that which creates reality. In one of my earliest publications on this subject, I wrote that "I wanted to investigate how the mind functions in the quantum mechanical field." When I look back at that now, I find that sentence a hollow phrase, for what is that quantum mechanical field? What do we really understand of quantum processes, and can they be interpreted as fields? As far as I know, the concept of a field came up when the phenomenon of electromagnetism was studied. That started with a simple observation of a compass needle which began to move when it was held close to a wire carrying an electric current. This observation wasn't understood, but was later included in a mathematical model. Because mathematics could describe the observation so well, the concept 'field' became generally accepted. But the field model is a function of time in this context because it takes into account the speed of light, while quantum processes seem to take place outside the speed of light. Concepts like 'consciousness field' inspire many people, but I wonder if the concept 'field' is right to describe the phenomena in which consciousness and reality 'impinge on each other,' because why would these phenomena or theories have to be described by a field?

Dick: This question certainly has to be asked. There has been a tremendous discussion about the interpretation of random number generator data in terms of 'energy.' A change in energy produces a field, but it is possible to interpret the same data in terms of information. The question is if information transfer can happen without energy. The non-local quantum correlations play a role in this as well. They seem to be without energy, but we haven't yet heard the last of that. Quantum correlations have to do with an undetermined state; in other words, a state in which they haven't yet been measured or observed. It is a system that doesn't exist yet, but it consists of everything which it potentially could become. There are two states: what it *may* become and what it *has* become. But does the transition between the two imply an increase of information? The field that someone like Lynne McTaggart means is the vacuum field, which is not really a field but a quantum mechanical phenomenon. According to the uncertainty relationship, particles (even in a vacuum) have to be continuously appearing and disappearing. That is the field according to her. What that would do in order to help us understand our will, I don't know.

Iebele: The connection that is made here, I think, is that information would be available forever if the exchange of information depended on non-locality. Ervin László simplified this idea into an understandable model, in which he said that information such as waves in an infinity without resistance — the vacuum field — will interfere with each other forever. He believed each new piece of information would forever remain recognizable as a unique pattern in this continuously growing complex field. People can, according to László, tune to this complex field to 'tap' information. He compared this to the Akasha records, some kind of intangible library of all knowledge. Our brains are not the carriers of information in this model, but function as an antenna for the available information that is 'stored' in this field. Conversely, the activity of our consciousness behaves like a transmitting station that sends out information. According to László, we add information to this field, through our actions as well as through our thinking. Information from the past, and possibly from the future, is supposed to be stored in this field.

Dick: David Bohm described an approach used in quantum mechanics in which a field appears. Bohm started his work in a peculiar way. He foresaw the enormous problems around the measurements of quantum processes and the role of consciousness in them. What he wanted was a physics that wasn't concerned with consciousness, which is why he wanted to get rid of the measurements; he found them too anthropocentric. His interpretation and mathematical handling of quantum mechanics contains something called 'quantum potential.' That, is a potential which is equally strong anywhere in space. Bohm solved the non-locality that always needs to be part of quantum mechanical models by describing a potential that doesn't decrease with distance. That potential changes itself according to the situation, and so it obtains the characteristics of a field. Later in life, Bohm turned 180 degrees, as he developed an interest in consciousness. For physical quantum phenomena, it's essential that we are not able to forecast in a developing system what the outcome will be of one single measurement; or, at least, that is the common interpretation. Nobel prize winner 't Hooft, however, still believes that a deterministic interpretation can be attributed to quantum physics. The discussion about whether fundamental chance exists is still going on. Most physicists interpret quantum formalism as a completely probabilistic outcome of potentiality. In fact, they say that at quantum level, we can only speak in terms of the development of possibilities and no longer of actuality because we don't know how actuality comes about. The transfer from potentiality to actuality, to reality, is in fact a magical and mysterious process.

Iebele: Even though one might seriously question why this would be the case, you make a connection between conscious behavior, like intentions, and the corresponding outcome of random number generators which, on the basis of the unpredictability of quantum phenomena, should be totally random.

Dick: I'm not the one to make that connection. That connection simply exists. The question is how to interpret it.

Iebele: Even if science sometimes disputes this heatedly, a popular interpretation inclines towards the idea that we are equipped with a creative consciousness, and that means quite a lot. The concept of creative consciousness takes one straight away to the area of the big life questions and ethics.

Dick: By wanting to explain this creative consciousness, one immediately provides an interpretation. What I like to do, and what is necessary in scientific work in my mind, is to separate the facts — research data — and the possible existential interpretation from each other.

Iebele: This interpretation still offers an explanatory model with which many people feel at home.

Dick: One of the five personality characteristics in psychology is openness, a sub-characteristic of which is being tolerance of ambiguity. Many people have a problem with this last one. They find it hard to live in a world in which things are multi-interpretable, and to have to live with uncertainty. As soon as science presents data in which there is a connection between intention and the behavior of matter, some people may over-interpret these data because they have a need for security. This, in fact, inhibits research, because it creates blinders.

Iebele: It could be that the need for certainty plays a role here, but maybe something else is a factor too. Apparently we observe our own consciousness, just like we perceive other things with other senses. We are aware of what we call consciousness, and we can even focus our consciousness on something to a certain extent. We can direct it. That is a certainty at the perceptual level. Our consciousness and the changes in it arise *because of* our consciousness; at least, that is how it seems to be.

Dick: The amusing thing about this, though, is that this perception — that we can make our own decisions — is debated fiercely by cognitive and neuropsychologists. They say that a person doesn't decide things of his own free will, but that his brain makes the decision. This theory is also supported by experiments that demonstrate that the brain (measured by means of EEGs) actually registers a certain activity — like bending a finger — before the subject consciously wants to execute it. The brain is faster than the will. This makes neuropsychologists say that a will of one's own does not exist.

Iebele: This way you approach people's conscious experience in an exclusively materialistic way by means of a whole range of measuring instruments. Such a method excludes everything that isn't physiologically measurable and then — using this as a basis — you formulate a model of how the brain and will interact. For many people, this method is too weak to rigidly proclaim that free will doesn't exist.

Dick: Yes, okay, but we can't deny the data from the kind of research I just mentioned, particularly as it can be reproduced. It is possible to ask questions about these data, however, and they may be explained in different ways. Libet himself, who did this research, said for example that the brain makes decisions, but that the experience of free will comes from somewhere else. Consciousness, according to him, can still pronounce a 'veto.' Consciousness says in fact something like "Your stupid brain decided this, but 'I' interfere and we will do it differently." An endless discussion may ensue about this, of course.

Iebele: Even if our actions were to be determined exclusively by our physical brain, the question still remains as to what the intelligence is behind this living system of our body and consciousness. In my opinion, that question is raised more urgently by REG experiments which show that intentions may influence material processes rather than by physiological research. The purely materialistic, deterministic model simply gives too little space to the rich experience of all kinds of inner sensation, and that's why I think people nowadays are looking for recognition of the non-material but active aspects of consciousness. If you recognize your own perceptions only partially in a model and the model doesn't acknowledge all other aspects of your perception at all, the question remains in the long run as to what extent that model serves the living, conscious being you experience yourself to be. Ultimately, we act using our frame of explanation. A materialistic model produces a materialistic world, I think.

Dick: That may not be totally true. Quantum mechanics produced non-local phenomena, something that is expressed exclusively between a number of 'individuals.' Consequently it surpasses the individual.

Iebele: That is exactly why I think quantum physics is embraced in the way it is nowadays. I think a collective awakening from the fuddle of individuality is taking place. Of course, every perception or discovery which supports this is jumped at, especially when it seems to come from hard, exact science that has partially introduced individualism. The communication between people has been improved by technology but, on the other hand, it has also decreased, precisely because technology has placed itself between people and nature. It may be a collective longing for society to comply again with a more natural, self-evident tuning to the environment. This applies to technology, too. I think many people long for science to find something which proves that a rich inner life fits within a deterministic model — or they long for a usable alternative model to present itself. I explicitly use present-day technology in my work to investigate if the present technological 'material' offers possibilities to open a window to the experience of interconnectedness, which is important for the development of an inner life, in my opinion.

Dick: I think that one of the most important things in our inner life is learning to deal with death. If we could prove that death isn't the absolute end, the social effect of that would be gigantic.

Iebele: The incredible impact any proof of life after death would have, evokes an enormous enthusiasm in me. In the time I was doing my first psychokinesis experiments, I started to make set-ups for intention experiments with a comparable enthusiasm. I thought at the time: if it were possible to use consciousness to make something move without touching it, it would be a tremendous experience, one that might lift me up above the boundary between life and death. Looking back, that may have been too high an expectation, but I certainly experienced my first experiments as miraculous. Until that time, I had only read about these experiments and I really hoped for a miracle when I tried to do them myself. At the beginning, the first series of artworks succeeded remarkably well, and I was euphoric about that. When I repeated such an experiment with other people present, however, the result was considerably less. I'm still trying to understand why my experiments in the beginning succeeded so well, and why I had lost the feeling of 'connectedness' a few months later when I repeated the experiments. Maybe the first series succeeded so well because of my enthusiasm or my receptivity to the results. That still gives me no idea about the actual mechanism behind this 'beginner's luck.'

Dick: There are two classes in the description of this kind of phenomena. The first one is physical, the second one is psychological. When you look from the psychological perspective, you could say that enthusiasm and the absence of fear of failure play a role, which makes it work better in the beginning than later: the so-called 'decline' effect. My hypothesis from a physical perspective is that as you get a better grip on these phenomena, you should be able to travel back in time, and then you encounter the 'grandfather paradox.' If you were able to travel back in time, you would be able to kill your grandfather when he was fifteen years old; in other words, before he became a father, let alone your grandfather. You can imagine that nature doesn't allow such paradoxes, and that may explain why you can't get a real grip on paranormal phenomena.

Don't touch the pendulum (2009)

Pendulum in bell, mounted on shock-free pedestal, 28 × 28 × 62 cm

Light, Coherence, and Consciousness

Conversation with Roeland van Wijk
Neuss, August 2009

Dr. Roeland van Wijk is a molecular cell biologist and biophysicist. He was vice president of the International Institute of Biophysics in Neuss (Germany), where he researches biophotons together with Fritz-Albert Popp. He is also involved with several projects in the area of integral and complementary medicine.

Iebele: In recent years, I have studied a variety of research results that have a certain influence on how we experience spirituality nowadays. The research on biophotons is one of these research areas. Biophotons are photons, light particles, that are emitted by biological systems. In the same manner, one could call the light from a light bulb 'light bulb photons.' Just as the light from a lamp tells us something about the nature of the lamp, biophotons obviously can give us information about the living system from which they originated.

Roel: A photon is a light particle, a packet of energy. Such a packet is able to escape because it has been stored away somewhere. The photon becomes a photon at the moment energy is released from a molecular construction, provided that the molecular construction is in a highly energetic state. Most of the time, energy of that kind stays within the cells of the body, where it plays a role in the processes of a living system. In the body, matter is constantly transferred from one kind of molecule into another. These are normal metabolic processes. Some transfers release energy; others need energy. Normally speaking, this transfer is in balance. Even if energy is involved in these processes, it is usually not enough to release a light particle. Much more energy is needed for that. In spite of this, our biological system does sometimes release light particles. We can't see these with the naked eye; there are too few of them. What we can do, however, is measure them. The fact that a body releases light particles means that certain bodily processes produce a large surplus of energy. These processes are connected with the fact that we use oxygen. Thanks to oxygen, we have small packets of energy at our disposal that can be used for metabolic processes. If something goes wrong, however, oxygen suddenly becomes the carrier of this large quantity of energy and that can be harmful. This surplus energy is then transferred to another molecule which is damaged in turn, causing the life processes to go out of balance. You can regard the living body as a molecular game, with the molecules constantly looking for balance in metabolic processes; a balance between the processes that need energy and those that give energy. Photons only leave the body when things go wrong in this game.

Iebele: If someone sends out few photons, that is a sign of good balance, good health, whereas if someone sends out many photons, the balance is lacking. That is an indication that processes in the body are functioning less well.

Roel: The breathing processes of the cells supply the packets of energy in the body, thanks to oxygen. When this process in the cells doesn't go smoothly, a photon is produced from the surplus energy. If processes in the body are well tuned to each other, you will find relatively few biophotons. If things get out of hand, however, the interactions in all kinds of processes change, and photons develop. The release of photons corresponds with the processes that are supposed to be tuned to each other and therefore they show a certain pattern. A healthy body produces little light, but shows characteristics of a high level of organization. As a system gets more disorganized, more energy will escape in the form of photons. In sick people, one sees a high intensity of photon emission, but a very low level of organization.

Iebele: The light a living being emits says something about the coherence, the organization of his biological system. The pattern in which light particles leaves the body contains the 'coding' of 'being alive,' as it were. The question is, of course, how you can discover this pattern.

Roel: If the photons we measure come from processes that are separate from each other, and if those processes have nothing to do with each other, then the pattern in this light is random. Suppose there are a thousand, separate, non-coherent processes; there is also no connection in time between the moments in which they generate a photon. At the moment that links develop among these thousand processes, however, just as in a biological system, then the release of photons will be connected.

Iebele: One could say that, if an organism is able to organize itself well, it has a different pattern of photon emission than an organism which is less good at doing that.

Roel: You notice that in photon emissions, because they become less chaotic. When the deviation from chance levels in biophoton emission increases in the course of time, this can be interpreted as a better organized, coherent system. The better a living system is organized, the more its photon emission pattern deviates from chance. Suppose everything in our body goes its own way, and nothing listens to each other, then that is a system that meets the chance expectation best. If that happens, something is really wrong. This is a hallmark of illness. On the other hand, when all processes are too tightly connected with each other, the system will become rigid. There is too much order and there is too little opportunity to adjust rapidly. That can lead to death as well. Living systems have a happy medium, and this is scrupulously maintained by a continuous exchange of energy among its various components.

Iebele: Apparently, not only the body of an organism is looking for a happy medium. Organisms look for that amongst themselves too. You did an experiment to study the photon emission of a single-celled organism. To measure its photon-emission, you put that single-celled organism in a light-tight box that is was completely closed off from the environment. There were two people in the room containing this experimental set up and you found that the photon emission of this single-celled organism showed correlations with the emotional state of these two people. That is remarkable to say the least, because there were no sensory stimuli that the single-celled organisms could react to. As I understand this experiment, transfer of information is therefore possible outside the 'senses.'

Roel: This was one of the first experiments in which we tried to find indications of 'field activity,' the existence of the influence of the

Flower of Life Studies #1: rigid system

White pencil and black board on foam, 52 × 52 cm,
Iebele Abel, 2009

Flower of Life Studies #2: coherent system

White pencil and black board on foam, 52 × 52 cm,
Iebele Abel, 2009

Flower of Life Studies #3: chaotic system

White pencil and black board on foam, 52 × 52 cm,
Iebele Abel, 2009

human consciousness on the biophotonic field of a living, single-celled organism. This experiment showed that in this way we may be able to study interconnectedness between living organisms.

Iebele: Because our body, and maybe our consciousness as well, is an interplay between chaos and coherence, I make a connection with the study of psychokinesis using random number generators. After all, these devices produce random signals. If your measurements of the pattern of biophoton emission deviate from chance, you interpret that as a sign of heightened coherence. In the same way, the deviation from chance expectation during 'intention experiments' is seen as an indication of interconnectedness between humans and matter in consciousness research..

Roel: You could say that at the moment I intentionally create a deviation in the REG, I pull it out of its random state, and I do that with my consciousness.

Iebele: You put life into a machine.

Roel: Yes, you transfer characteristics of a living system to a non-living system. One could look at the REG data as if it were a living system, by using the same method we use to analyze a living system. That is done rarely or not at all in psychic research, as far as I know.

Iebele: No, I haven't heard much about that either. It is interesting to bring those fields closer together, I think. I started to work with REGs in order to study the interaction between consciousness and physical reality because life or, more specifically, consciousness interests me. It then goes without saying that I look at biological systems too. One of the things that is characteristic of consciousness is, of course, memory, and that is what research into biophotons is engaged in too.

Roel: One cannot record things until they are very well tuned to each other. The neural network can only record something if you are able to repeat a situation. Now a situation can only be repeated if the neural network finds itself in a constant environment. That's why it is of the utmost importance for the brain to have an absolutely constant temperature. If you look at fish, for example, their memory is limited. In their environment, the temperature changes all the time. Fish are cold-blooded animals and can't adjust their own temperature. The temperature of their brain changes constantly. The more an organism can stabilize its temperature, the more it can record.

Iebele: As humans, we are reasonably able to regulate our comfort. Our bodies not only keep the brain temperature nice and constant, but we can also change our environment ourselves. When it is cold outside, we turn up the heating. Thus, modern comforts allow us to live in a 'warm bath' that varies little in temperature. I can imagine that our memory increases and our consciousness is raised because we are able to make our lives more stable.

Roel: Yes, you will have more functions that you can record.

Iebele: What I find mysterious, is that we are conscious of our own consciousness. We have a metaconsciousness. I wonder how that could have arisen.

Roel: It is certainly fascinating that we are becoming more and more conscious. Our ability to react gets more and more differentiated, and it is stored in memory, too. The capacity to remember increases in this way as well. There are models of consciousness relating to biophotons that relate consciousness to coherence. But what is an optimal coherence? It isn't a maximal coherence, for sure, because that leads to death. We may evolve to a higher degree of coherence, but that means the range of our reactions decreases. We are able to react more precisely, but in a smaller area.

Iebele: The interplay between being coherent and noncoherent, which is how it works in biological systems, seems to be at work in daily life, too. The way in which our bodies function at a molecular level may be associated with the way we, as human beings, deal with each other and with nature. Looking for the happy medium between freedom and alliance, give and take, chaos and order; that process is the order of the day, isn't it? When we strive for order, we give up freedom. The stronger one focuses on order, the more rigid the system becomes in which we live together. It becomes less and less flexible. Technology and social systems that have to be preserved to guarantee a steady living environment require a lot of time and work, meaning a lot of freedom seems to be lost.

Roel: I see that happening already. We have to take more and more measures to survive. Humankind keeps inventing more ways to keep its environment more stable. That's how it weakens itself, and it has to do a lot of work to make and keep the environment constant. In that constant environment, greater coherence becomes possible, but where will it end? We can only speculate about that. Maybe we are forgetting something. Maybe there is something we just can't see yet with our present consciousness, but that would change the picture completely if we could.

Iebele: We have made images of umbellifers today by putting them in a light-tight box. With an advanced machine, a photon counter, you can see how such a flower emits light. It shows a very different reality. It is a different filter on reality. In your portrait that I used for a study, it is even more visible than in the flowers. The eyes are very dark. The processes there are obviously more coherent than at the mouth and throat, which radiate more light. So far we only knew about images of incident and reflecting light. That is the only reality that we saw until now, and that is registered by photographers and artists. In spite of this, there has always been an idea of radiating light, the halo or the light body, for example. One cannot see such images with the eyes, although you may wonder how the halo and the light body were ever added to our idiom. Some people see auras, and paint them too. That may be quite different from biophotons, but anyway there is now a technique available to make radiating light visible. Such images change our consciousness; it makes our image of reality a little more complete. And then it is true, of course, that one such photon, which causes a dot on a photo, has in fact an extraordinarily complex origin. Such a photon is the result of a complex process in the biological system, in this case an umbellifer, about one inch in size. The image of such a flower contains a cognitive aspect; the image is caused by the way in which we look at the world in our culture.

Roel: In fact you are looking at a different world, but you don't know yet what that world will produce. If you look in an electromagnetic way, as we have been able to do so far, much gets lost too. You can see that from the photos we have made this afternoon. You see something in them, but there is a lot you can't see. We are used to seeing the details of everything of course; we normally just look at small form changes. We often forget that behind those form changes that usually appear relatively slowly, there is an enormous vibration. You start to experience the reality of this vibration by seeing the images of it.

Vibrations of 9 flowers

Giclée print on dibond, 90 × 90 cm,
Iebele Abel, 2009

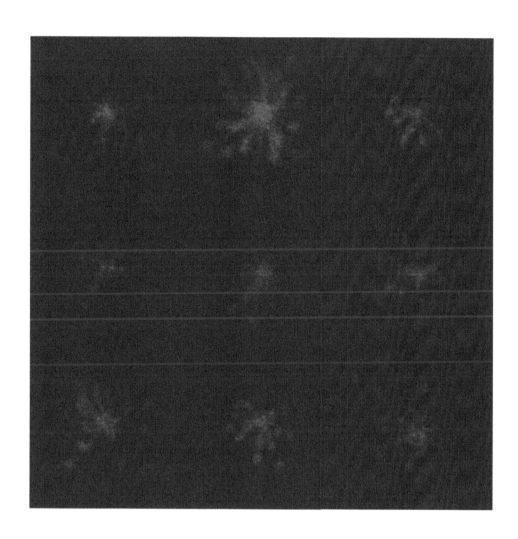

Study for self portrait without a Lightsource

Giclée print on dibond, 90 × 90 cm,
Roeland van Wijk, Tohoku Institute of Technology, Sendai Japan,
Iebele Abel, 2009

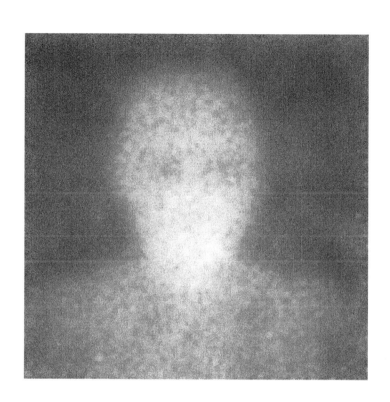

Acknowledgments

Thank you,

Hans Gerding for our wonderful conversations. You have been invaluable to me over the past years. Dick Bierman for your patience and the love for your profession. Ingrid Rollema for your love and freedom. Brenda Dunne for your clarity. Roger Nelson for your hospitality and your enthusiasm. Robert Jahn for your words and your fondness for animals. Jacco Lamfers for close to 40 years of friendship and for your music. Peter Groen for working with me on a project with an uncertain outcome. Tijn Touber for lending me a hand all those years. Roeland van Wijk for opening up new pathways. Peter van Kan for creating that good atmosphere in which everything can be said. Peter Blok, because you are a friend. Nelki Louret and Gerard van Bussel for the telephone calls that sometimes lasted a very long time. Dineke Huizenga because you're always willing to think things through with me. Tom Huizenga for initiating this book. Jessica de Boer for your outstanding comments. Henri Nijenhuis and Marianne van Delft for correcting the manuscript. Hanneke van Alphen and Ineke Raeskin for transcribing. Janneke Kronemijer and Roelof Nanninga for your support over a lifetime. Ankie, you are the basis of so many things. Armijn Woudman for the graphical design of this book. Lindsey Housden because of your willingness to be the first female Preacher. Martin Zwaan for the great care you took of my work. Greg Ward, where would I be without *radiance*? Hermien van Sloten for the translation. Gwendolyn Holstege, for the really good interview which, nevertheless, didn't appear in this publication. Sjoukje Reijenga, for frankly sharing your work experiences. Jan van Toorn for the great years we spent in this jungle together. Noel Ross-Russell for mind gardening. Rino Wong Chung for the 'crucial' meetings in Antwerp. Paul de Blot for teaching gratitude. Judith, Joris, and the animals, thanks for the good life we have at home together.

Thanks to all friends and colleagues, for your enthusiasm and support. *Stroom The Hague* granted a research fund.

CPSIA information can be obtained at www.ICGtesting.com
Printed in the USA
BVOW10s0242270314

348907BV00003B/6/P

9 781936 033072